# Down Home

*America's Country Decorating Book*

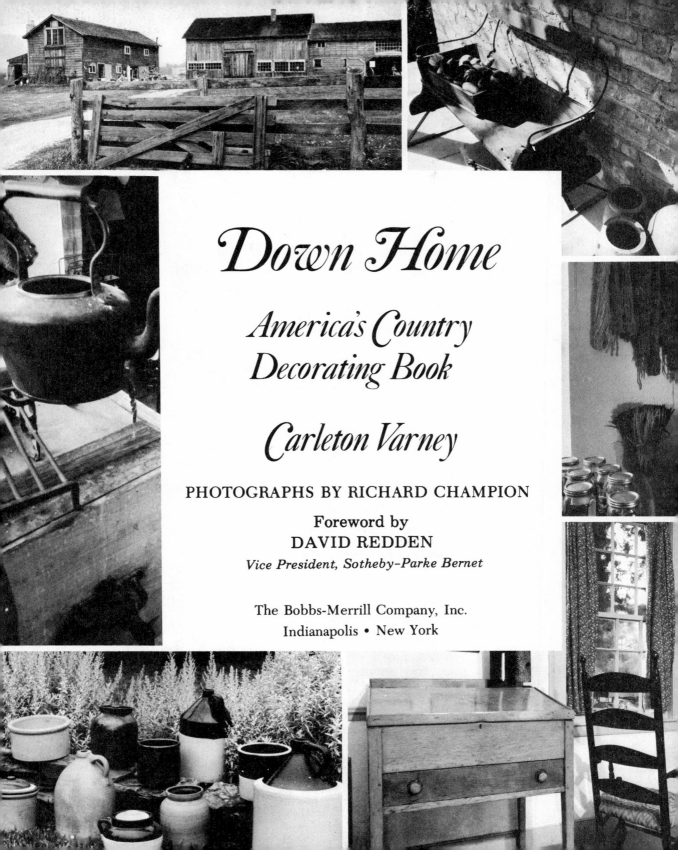

# Down Home

## America's Country Decorating Book

## Carleton Varney

### PHOTOGRAPHS BY RICHARD CHAMPION

Foreword by
**DAVID REDDEN**
*Vice President, Sotheby-Parke Bernet*

The Bobbs-Merrill Company, Inc.
Indianapolis • New York

*Other Books by Carleton Varney*

You and Your Apartment
The Family Decorates a Home
Carleton Varney's Book of Decorating Ideas
Carleton Varney Decorates Windows
Decorating with Color
Decorating for Fun
Carleton Varney Decorates from A to Z
Be Your Own Decorator
There's No Place Like Home

Copyright © 1981 by Carleton Varney

All rights reserved, including the right of reproduction
in whole or in part in any form.
Published by The Bobbs-Merrill Company, Inc.
Indianapolis New York

**Library of Congress Cataloging in Publication Data**

Varney, Carleton.
  Down home.

  1. Interior decoration—United States.
2. Antiques in interior decoration.
3. Decoration and ornament, Rustic—United States. I. Title.
NK2002.V3     747.213     81-66316
ISBN 0-672-52692-1        AACR2

Designed by Marcia Ben-Eli
Manufactured in the United States of America

First printing

For my sons, Nicholas, Seamus and Sebastian,
and for my wife, their Mommy, Suzanne . . .
they who walk the fields and hills with me—DOWN HOME.

Without the kind assistance of the many friends who permitted me—and cameras—into their charming homes, this book would never have been a reality. I am most grateful to these people who enjoy and live with the Down Home style:

Ruth Gordon Ellis, Mr. and Mrs. John Wade Bell III, Kinsey Bell, Mrs. Jane Mitchell, Mr. and Mrs. Lawson Hamilton, Carol and Donald Campbell, Brian and Joanne White, Amelia and Dan Musser, Julia Child, Richard Katzenberger, Joe Lang, Suzie and Elliott Clarke, and Paul Chaleff.

I also acknowledge with gratitude the help given me by the White House staff, by White House social secretary Mrs. Gretchen Poston, and by Mrs. Rosalynn Carter.

I am delighted to show in this book the 1981 Victorian Christmas Tree.

For their constant help in the preparation of this book, I thank Catherine Revland, Rosalind Cole, Irene Frank, Jim Tschantre, Marcia Ben-Eli, Linda Worden and my editor, Grace Shaw.

Special thanks also go to Phil Porter of the Mackinac Island State Park Commission, and to the friends of the Lewisburg Foundation of Lewisburg, West Virginia.

And to the greatly talented Richard Champion, who traveled about the country with me to take the pictures for *Down Home*, I say thank you for our years of friendship.

Carleton Varney
Hillandale Farm
April 1981

# Contents

# Foreword

Carleton Varney, with his wide-ranging sympathy for the way we live or want to live, has caught up a new thread of the American Dream: the need of so many of us to have a haven in our lives for simplicity and honesty and tradition, for communion with past and nature. As I wield my gavel over countless auctions in New York and elsewhere, I see this almost palpable yearning expressed in the fierce competition amongst frantic bidders for the relics of our rural past. For we are the inheritors of our forefathers' ineluctable drift from the countryside, lured away by glittering city dreams of advancement and luxury; and while we admire their courage in forsaking their old ways, we regret the loss of place, of ancestral homes, fields and hills, of peace and stillness, for which now more than ever we turn again home, Down Home. Down Home—a mood, a style, a sensibility; and not for the rural returned only, for city folk are putting the country into the city; and rocking horses, quilts and blanket chests ascend city elevators as high-rise apartments go Down Home.

And yet this appetite for our country past is not difficult to indulge. All the new-fangled collecting interest has only encouraged saving and selling, so that the antique marketplace is brimming with antique paraphernalia, whether it's called Americana, folk art, or just rustical whimsies. Search out tag sales, the well-stocked antique shop, and country auctions. Local papers are the guide, and I especially recommend the many regional weeklies and monthlies. But don't overlook bargains in the city. Perhaps, as you would expect, the country look is often cheaper in the city, especially if the look is not Monticello high-style.

But navigate carefully. Each purchase should be a lesson in discrimination, an education in the signposts for quality. Train your eye to see the subtleties of fine craftsmanship and artistic worth. For you will have to depend on your eye to cull out the fraud and the fake, to reveal the hopelessly restored ("like new") and the haplessly repaired. Read up, subscribe to good magazines (*Antiques*, for example), talk to the dealers, and go to museums and historical societies. The largest auction houses hold major "Americana" sales which are a must, if you can get to them, for learning current prices and for developing your eye by touching (essential, but what museum lets you?) as well as seeing some of the best antiques available on the market.

And that is the way to get value. Which, right now, means ever increasing value. Let's not buy antiques simply as an investment (too crude!), but let's not quarrel with a situation which allows us, if we have a good eye, to indulge our love of beauty with a clear conscience. For are we not putting money into our purses? If not for ourselves, then for our descendants? Having our cake and eating it too? Maybe not, but who can resist this sort of sophistical justification for a series of sizable expenditures?

Not that buying for Down Home need be expensive. Plain country furniture still costs no more than reproductions. Simple country paintings can be a bargain, especially naïve landscapes and those innumerable nineteenth-century portraits of all our collective ancestors. Fanatical quilts cost far less than the effort expended in stitching them warrants. Discover how easy it is to put together an exciting collection of Staffordshire figures, coin silver spoons, early trade signs, or copper-mounted cooking tools. There is still lots of everything.

And as you collect, recollect. What does the past mean to you? What carries resonance for you? For that's what you want to surround yourself with, not with an artificial accumulation of objects. "Be you!" says Carleton Varney. That's the way to living and decorating Down Home style, and this beautiful book is your guide.

> "Home is where one starts from. . . .
> And the end of all our exploring
> Will be to arrive where we started
> And know the place for the first time."
>
> T. S. Eliot
>
> *David Redden*
> *Vice President, Sotheby–Parke Bernet*

# Down a Country Road

"We may build more splendid habitations,
Fill our rooms with paintings and with sculptures,
   But we cannot
Buy with gold the old associations!"

*Henry Wadsworth Longfellow*
The Golden Milestone

This book is about country living—the kind of living that we call Down Home. Defining it will take all these pages and dozens of photographs, because Down Home is not a decorating style that can be ordered by number; it is a multifaceted look that encompasses the past as well as the present. It employs nature's own clear, pure colors and honest textures. More than a look or a line, it is also a fragrance, a mood. It is an awakening of your own private and most pleasant sense memories—the gold of Longfellow's "old associations."

Understanding Down Home begins with a drastic shift in pace. Most country things are likely to meander rather than to catapult, to wind rather than to rush, to fall in graceful curves and scallops. Line loses its tension in the country. It loosens and stretches and winds down. Speed in the country is likely to be nothing more than Godspeed.

"I often see flowers from a passing car
That are gone before I can tell what they are."

Follow the road slowly enough to see what kinds of flowers Robert Frost saw
only as a blur.

From ocean to ocean, the American country home is often down a wind-
ing road, a series of inward turns from freeway to highway to county road to
country lane to Down Home. As we draw near, we roll down the windows,
take a deep breath, stretch, sigh, and exhale the last of the city air from our
lungs.

Many a depleted city dweller uses the transition on the road from city to
country as a time to shed city anxieties. The goal is to run into the homestead
already in a state of tranquillity, already in a frame of mind to put aside the
thought of time as a series of urgent appointments.

"Do this, buy now, go here,
Stand up, come down . . ."

Carl Sandburg's description of city living is all too familiar to most of us. Appointments are for the city. The city is bold: full of verve, din, and dash. It is
hard-edged, artificial, electrifying, opulent, dynamic—Saturday Night Fever
all week long. City decorating styles can be any or all of the above.

Life is at its zestful best when it has contrasts, and many people want two
kinds of living: the city to recharge their batteries; the country to provide
peace, harmony, and a continuity with the past.

In the country the past is everywhere, and the future is little more than a
dream of apples; a yearning for the first snow or the first crocus, the first
trout. In the country, the ever changing seasons are enough change. The difference in pace is everywhere; the difference exists even in line. City line is
rectangular or square—jutting lines and forty-five-degree turns, a no-time-to-
linger tautness. Country line is more round than square, a slow bombé, a
wide circling.

Of course the country can be stimulating too, but it doesn't so much shock
as startle. The sight of one prematurely red branch flashing amid the
greenery may make the heart skip a beat, but it never jolts the system. People
don't want to be shocked in the country. They don't want to find a large
vinyl hand where the sofa used to be. They don't want to throw their coats
over a row of paintbrushes dipped in liquid plastic and stuck to the wall.

*A country swing for two is inviting—either under a spreading chestnut tree or on the family porch.*

Such whimsy may be fine in the city, but country whimsy is more likely to be a naughty Victorian boot pull or a pie safe gaily poked full of holes.

Down Home may be off the New England seacoast, in an Appalachian valley surrounded by prairie wheat, lying under the desert sun, or tucked into the pine forests of the Cascade mountains. It may be a cozy saltbox, a rugged log cabin, a Victorian farmhouse, a mountain A-frame, or a rambling ranch or adobe house with a central courtyard. It may be made of stone, wood, or clay. It may have one room, or ten, or twenty-two. For all their differences, Down Home country houses share certain similarities: they are honest and usually modest. They have a warmth, a simple beauty, and a look of comfort that puts people at peace with the world and makes them all of a sudden very hungry.

Down Home rooms are filled with utilitarian objects of beauty. There is more likely to be a nosegay of Queen Anne's lace on the hall table than a bouquet of hothouse roses. The house has a special fragrance, compounded of polished wood, something good baking, drying herbs, a fresh breeze. The sounds that fill the air are those of laughter, of the steaming kettle, and of the ancestral clock chiming away the hours.

City satisfaction may lie in a pay raise, another lap around the reservoir, or getting through one more week without a major catastrophe. Country satisfaction lies in a full pantry, snug walls, a high woodpile, and a gathering of hungry people around the big dining table. From room to room, serenity reigns. No shocking colors here. No stark whites, no clutter of purposeless ornaments. The past—the best of the past—is all around. That past has a certain glow, not a surface city-slicker shine but a patina that comes from being old and Quality. The most successful Down Home rooms are furnished with the "real thing" and pulled together with nature's own colors and textures so that there is no jarring note upon crossing the threshold: what the eye meets within never clashes with what is without.

So far, Down Home has been defined in intangibles—feelings, fragrances, moods, remembrances. This book will supply the specifics of country home decorating, but you yourself will need to make the choices about what elements of the past you want to preserve and live with, to enjoy. Down Home is never a reproduction of the past but a combination of what we choose to be reminded of and the best of what is technologically modern. Complicated? Not at all—and more satisfying than you could ever anticipate.

Only the most Spartan purist would want to return to the life of our forebears, a life of horsehair and outhouses, frigid rooms in the winter and no refrigeration in the summer. Although we don't envy them the hard life they endured, we do want to recapture the good of what they had—or at least what we think they had and feel we lack. But before we try to translate that heady intangible into a decorating scheme, it will be helpful to take a look at how most Americans really did live in the good old days.

The house probably faced the sun for maximum light, for the rooms were small and were dimly lit only at night by candle or oil flame. Perhaps the skeletal structure of the house showed—exposed beams, rafters or brick. It had a dirt floor, unless its occupants, blessed by fortune, were able to lay down wood. It had an enormous fireplace, perhaps as wide as eight feet, located centrally to provide maximum heat. In the corner was a brick oven where the daily bread was baked.

For untold generations, ordinary folk lived in houses whose fireplace was the focus of a room in which all the functions of cooking, eating, living, working and sleeping went on. That main room was called the keeping room, the place where people kept warm and kept each other company.

Beyond the central living quarters were the beds. They may have been placed in a corner of the one big room, on a loft under the rafters, or in a separate bedroom if the family was able to afford such a luxury. The beds were high, well off the floor and away from drafts. They were piled with feather comforters and as many as five patchwork quilts in the wintertime, since the house was additionally poorly insulated. The windows rattled and the wind blew in between the chinks no matter how much dirt or snow was heaped high against the north side of the house. When family members rose on winter mornings, there was often ice in the washbowl. They dressed quickly and hurried to the kitchen, where there was warmth as well as the smell of coffee and sputtering sausages.

In this or any other country today, one's finest furniture and accessories are usually displayed in the living room. So it was in our ancestors' day, too—provided our typical farm family of yesterday had a parlor at all. If they did, it was a rather stiff and formal place used only when company came. The sofa and chairs were simply not built to sink back into, shoes off, feet up. The parlor, or "best room," was a place where people perched on the edges of their chairs, drank tea, and acted respectable while entertaining important visitors. In the winter, the room was the coldest as well as the least inviting place to be, since the door was kept closed to conserve heat in the rest of the house.

The kitchen was most likely a roomy place, although never big enough for all the living that went on in it. The cooking area had a dry sink that contained pans of water for cooking and washing. (The dry sink was misnamed: it was a wet arrangement.) Much of the cooking was done in the fireplace, although the family may have owned a wood stove as well. Baking was done in the brick oven in the winter, and, if the family had an outdoor oven, outside in the summer.

As many as three generations probably mingled in the keeping room. A dropleaf table may have helped to create a little more room between meals, but if the family was large, conditions were undeniably crowded.

Much of the productive household activity went on in this one room: father and sons mending harness, grandfather turning a spindle, grandmother weaving a rag rug, mother doing the mending, children their lessons, daughters their dowry needlework. This was a house with few secrets; privacy meant retreating to a cold, dark part of the house.

Behind the house was the privy. Using it could never have been delightful, and in the wintertime it was an ordeal, especially at night. Just contemplating the cold dash to and from that dark, unheated place was chilling enough. A chamberpot was kept under the bed for the faint of heart.

The house was crowded above as well as below. All sorts of objects hung from the rafters: vegetables, herbs, fruit, baskets, implements. And since there were no closets, people stored their few personal belongings overhead or in chests.

In these overcrowded rooms, babies were born, old people died, young people courted, brothers and sisters argued, and life went on. Cabin fever raged in January, February and March, when the long weeks of isolation, confinement, and lack of privacy began to take their toll. But spring always came, and life expanded again to the outdoors. People ate supper on the lawn, visited neighbors, and worked in the fields. Confinement to the house, dimming in memory, made warm weather living all the sweeter. . . .

This sketch has more accurately described rural life than do the cheerful scenes of Currier and Ives or Grandma Moses. When times were hard, people suffered; when they were happy, people remembered. What we remember today is an old stirring, older than we are, of belonging to a place; the closeness of the family; the satisfaction of self-sufficiency; the fulfillment of the simple expectations of health and harmony. Those are the feelings we want to re-create in a country place of today. And how fortunate we are to have, along with a rich heritage to draw on, such wonderful modern conveniences as central heating, indoor plumbing, and the light bulb, to say nothing of telephones, Betamaxes, hot tubs, and Cuisinarts!

Down Home is simply this: the best of the past with modern conveniences. Each home is unique, for individual memories cannot be duplicated. The late-twentieth-century country dweller sits by the fire after dinner with a glass of blackberry brandy perhaps, sinks into soft pillows, and looks contentedly around at the luster of old wood while he listens to soft music, soft voices.

"This is my life," says the country dweller to the room at large. "This is who I am." Down Home living means being part of a house that is in turn a part of nature. This is truly rooting oneself to the earth; it is one of the reasons why we are so drawn to country living in this age of uncertainty.

Many people resist "going country" because of their aversion to "Early American," a decorating style that uses ersatz pieces to mass-produce the look of a bygone era. True Down Home country style is no more like that artificial duplication of American country living than an electric fire is like a real one. Fortunately, that style is steadily being replaced by true country pieces as Americans continue to rediscover the beauty of their own past.

"You can't come back to a home unless it was a home you went away from."

*Carl Sandburg*

*This Norman lantern has distinct appeal—and the rose hips growing about it add just the right amount of natural country spice.*

The country road is a special place, designed for leisurely, appreciative travel. The fences, the hedges, the blueberry bushes, the apple trees, the mailboxes, the bird houses, the smell of honeysuckle—all offer the traveler the best of nature. The country road also offers the best of nature's design, and folk with an eye out for country style will surely find inspiration along the road. The barn reds and the whites of country houses might provide you with color-scheme inspiration for either the outside or the inside of your house. Or perhaps you'll be turned on by a house painted a gray-green with white trim and black shutters. A country house painted soft yellow with white trim is always inviting, too. Assuredly, somewhere along the country road, you'll find a barn, weathered in the country manner, that will give you an idea for the family room.

Country roads are lined nowadays with charming antique shops, and within them you are likely to find treasures to grace your living room— maybe an old cow weathervane to hang on the wall above the fireplace, or a mallard duck decoy or two to use as bookends. For a table centerpiece, you may come across an old basket to use as a flower or plant container. The country road leads to a wealth of such things for lovers of things Down Home. Look and ye shall find.

*Along the country road, stop at a carriage barn for design inspirations.*

Along the country road, you might even come across a pair of Cotswold stone planters, favorites for generations. Fill them with sedum.

The homemade pine toolbox is a family heirloom. If you don't want it for tools, use it as a bird feeding station or for holding bunches of country asters.

*Country roads say barns and fences and a profusion of morning glories.*

*Nasturtiums, hollyhocks and brown wicker furniture make the end of a road delightful, as do country benches under a tree and stockpiles of wood for the winter ahead.*

# Country Style

"How do you do, my farmer friend?"
"Howdy."
"Nice-looking country you have here."
"Fer them that likes it."
"Live here all your life?"
"Not yit."

How does Down Home style differ from all others? The answer requires breaking down "style" into components of color, texture, line, and even fragrance.

For comparison's sake, let's look at the grandness of the French court of Louis XV. In a word, the style was ornate; but specifically, in color it was gold, white, blue and/or pale pink. In texture it was watered silk moiré and flocked velvet. In line it was curved, scrolled, and encrusted, with curliqued legs on chairs and tables. In fragrance it was blood-red roses and pomander.

Down Home style, by contrast, is the color of blackberry, golden birch, and cardinal's wing. It is furry mullein leaf, nubby rag carpet, and smooth old wood. Its line is also curved, but in nature's gentler arcs, combined with many straight-and-simple lines. Its fragrance is cooling bread, bayberry and applewood fire. While Louis Quinze was the style of kings and queens, Down

Home is the style of hollyhocks along the wall, as honest and straightforward as Carl Sandburg's farmer friend who introduces this chapter.

First, color . . .

"Let eyes that ache come here and look," wrote that great advocate of country life, Henry David Thoreau; and color can indeed be a balm that heals the aching city eye. A simple rule: if a color doesn't exist in nature, don't use it. Then you can take advantage of another rule: nature's colors never clash. Of course the home decorator can't bring all of nature's colors indoors; selecting the right combination is half the fun.

A country house is no place for beefed-up "decorator" colors, those jazzy shades that come and go. One year it's plum, the next avocado; but neither color ever looks like nature's own. Also avoid the electric shades, those that look like traffic lights or neon. Leave them behind in the city, along with disco colors, Day-Glo, and any shade that looks as if it might glow in the dark. Such shocking colors are too jarring in the tranquil setting of a country home.

But earth colors are too drab, you say? How about the yellow of a buttercup, the blue of a bachelor's button, or exuberant zinnia red? From the startling to the restful, nature's palette will provide the country decorator with enough choices to create any desired mood.

Country elegance? Listen to John Greenleaf Whittier:

"As spring the winter doth succeed
And leaves the naked trees do dress,
The earth all black is clothed in green
At sunshine each their joy express."

Spring green, wet earth, and sun yellow: a bit of diligent searching will yield colors that duplicate nature's own elegant spring scheme.

Simplicity?

"There is the house, with the gate red-barred,
  And the poplars tall;
And the barn's brown length, and the cattle-yard,
  And the white horns tossing above the wall."

Another winning Whittier color combination: barn red, silvery green, weathered brown, and the ivory of cow's horns.

*When decorating in the Down Home way, choose fabrics dyed with natural pigments. The colors in the yarns hanging here came from nature's own dye pots—leaves, fruits, flowers, vegetables, barks and roots.*

Something dramatic?

> "There are horses neighing on far-off hills,
> tossing their long white manes,
> and mountains flash in the rose-white dusk
> their shoulders black with rains . . ."

Pale dusky rose, a flash of creamy white, and the muted black and green of the horizon.

But you say you want something a little more vivid, warmer and more voluptuous?

> "These fallen hazelnuts,
> stripped late of their green sheaths,
> grapes; red-purple,
> their berries dripping with wine,
> pomegranates already broken . . ."

Nature as described through the awe and wonder of the poet is more than enough color inspiration; but in order to successfully duplicate that crushed berry shade, you will probably have more luck matching your expectations if you choose a fabric for your couch or pillow that is one of nature's own, and even greater success if the natural fabric is dyed with natural pigments.

> "A color stands abroad
> on solitary hills
> That science cannot overtake
> but human nature *feels*."

Emily Dickinson never saw colors made in a chemical soup. Consequently, she wasn't faced with the dilemma of trying to achieve colors that match nature's own. We are. But if you will stick to wool, cotton, linen and other natural fibers, you will avoid many offending hues. Sharpening your eye to nature's true, pure colors is another way to make the selection easier and more successful. We begin with the color nature yields most abundantly: yellow.

Since it can be made from so many of nature's pigments, it's no surprise that yellow was popular in American rural life during those many years when fibers were dyed at home with pigments extracted from leaf, fruit, flower, vegetable, bark and root. The lowly onionskin produced a yellow from pale gold to rust. Other sources were lady's purse, lichen, sagebrush, osage orange, mushrooms, goldenrod, mullein, milkweed, marigolds. The yellow palette produced by these natural pigments ranged from cream to buttercup to ripe wheat to amber to rust to umber.

So—country yellow can be as bright as saffron, as orange as a carrot, or as leaden as a sky before a storm. But always it must glisten!

What other color could be more appropriate in the country than green? Nature's own greens have a depth that seems to have light behind it. Some greens were made from pigments of the juiciest, greenest leaves. Citron green was made from the leaves of asters, privet, and heather. Other greens, particularly the deeper, more metallic shades, were made from non-green leaves such as purple coleus. Pine needles in an iron pot produced a sensational olive, snapdragons a pale, soft green, and purple foxglove a clear chartreuse. Lupine produced a grassy green. Often an article being dyed was given a final dip into an indigo vat to enrich and intensify the green.

Green is also nature's cover-up color, the one that masks all those glorious reds, oranges, and yellows in the leaves until it's time for the chlorophyll to exit through the stems, to return the following year. Green is quite literally nature's lifeblood. From the pale, clear green of early spring, made from lily of the valley leaves, to the full-bodied green of midsummer, made with blue lupine and ageratum, to the silvery green of midwinter, made with seaweed, nature's ever changing color scheme offers the home decorator an endless array of clear, honest country hues.

Blues to purples are another group of colors made from an abundance of nature's raw ingredients. A pale hue came from dipping fibers into a dye made from red and purple hollyhock petals, or from crushed blueberries, wild grapes or blackberries. But for the clear, cool, intense blue that is as American as the flag and the blue jean, the dye was made from the indigo plant, which was chopped up and allowed to rot in water under the sun until it was reduced to a smelly paste. A sky blue resulted from the first dip; further exposure produced a dusky blue; then that wonderful intense indigo blue, a color some claim cannot be duplicated synthetically. Colors born in a chemical soup pot are sometimes too loud and insistent—lacking the depth that came from many dippings.

From blue to slate (a favorite country decorating color, especially in the Northeast) to dusky mauve and other twilight hues . . . in nature, no color is boring, least of all gray. Even this most subdued of nature's colors can be alive with light. The dusk at Thanksgiving time is a phantom shade of purple-hued gray that many a country stroller would love to duplicate on a wall. Snow in shadow, the silvery gray of a weatherbeaten barn door, the dramatic gray of an impending Dakota cloudburst—how could anyone claim that gray is boring? The herbal dyer achieved gray by dipping fabric in a mixture made from sunflower seeds, the green shoots of blackberry bushes, rhododendron leaves or the rosy stain of the mulberry fruit.

A total absence of color is too stark in a Down Home room. Even snow is not the dead white used so often in the city to create the illusion of light and space. In the country we can do without illusions. Liven up white with a bit of raspberry, a hint of citron. Cream, ivory, mushroom, and the color of unbleached wool are all preferable to bleached-bone white.

And now for nature's most glorious color, red. Country reds range from pale maple to the rich ruby of the elderberry, heavy with juice. Traditionally, red dye was made from red substances: flower petals, fruit juices, beets, red beans, bloodroot, or wild black cherry root. The brightest and most desired red came not from a plant, however, but from an insect, the cochineal. This is the red of redcoats. Just as appropriate to a Down Home room would be the crimson of the cardinal or the scarlet tanager. Nature uses red sparingly, for the most part, but she also uses it for her most theatrical displays. The flare of a sunset on a hillside of flaming sumac and maple is nature pulling out all the red stops.

As nature indulges in drama, so may the country decorator. Just be sure the red is a true country one, the kind that looks as if the sun were behind it. Getting red into a room can be as simple as framing the sunset with chairs grouped at a window. Or you might throw a bright Indian rug, with astonishing lightning bolts of red, over a bed or a balcony so that in the sunshine it looks as if it had been dyed by dipping skeins of wool into an Arizona sunrise.

*Herbs can be dried in any room of the house. A simple and practical year-round accessory for the herb gardener, this pine rack with pegs hangs in a country kitchen above the cookbook shelf.*

For more subtlety, there are many natural reds in hues from delicate pink to rich coral.

A knowledgeable dyer knew where to find a lichen that produced a bright pink and another that yielded a magenta, as well as a dark yellow mushroom that rendered a deep, glorious salmon. The sometimes poisonous Russula yielded a pink the color of the inside of a shell. Other berries and herbs produced shades that ranged from tender flower pink to the maroon of Indian corn.

For the color of the earth itself, the natural dyer used brown materials: acorn and butternut hulls, beech leaves, the bark of the osage orange. Shades in the brown family ran from the light, tawny mushroom that came from sumac seeds to the deep rich brown of wet soil, which was made from black walnuts and further deepened by the addition of a rusty nail to the dye pot.

Country living sharpens the eye as it slows us down, and this new sensitivity to color should be reflected in your decorating scheme. As Robert Frost observed, the faster you travel, the less you see. Raspberries ripening just beyond the roadside ditch aren't even a faint blur to someone driving by, but for those who like to walk a country road in midsummer, it's hard *not* to keep an eye out for those plump little rubies hidden among the leaves. Other country accents also require a sharp eye—the flash of a tanager or the blur of a blue jay. Fleeting little surprises of bright color also liven up a country house. Turn a corner, and there's a scattering of crimson or delphinium-blue pillows on a bed. A frugal bit of coral stitched into the somber design of a treasured patchwork quilt may generate more interest than might a liberal use of that rich color.

It is not enough, however, to depend only on a pillow for color. Color accents must also be spotted elsewhere in a room—on an upholstered stool, perhaps, or in one of the roses in a floral-and-stripe wallpaper. The russet of the grapes in the stenciled border on page 208 is also used on the doors. This approach to color is called accessory decorating, and nothing could be more appropriate in a country house. Gone are the days when everything had to match. Such a look was safe, perhaps—as safe as it was boring. People used to worry about combining colors that didn't "go together," and avoided red and green, or blue and yellow, for fear of showing poor taste. The country decorator has been freed from unnecessary fret about using that stripe with this print and a solid.

One of the reasons why color is so important in a Down Home setting is the necessity for a house to harmonize with the out-of-doors. In summer you don't want your house to be drab by comparison, and in winter you want it to be a cheerful contrast to nature's somber cold-weather apparel. Fortunately, it is no longer considered gauche to live with lots of color.

Can't one really heap on too much color, though? Surely. But the secret of avoiding too much of a good thing is to unify the show of color by means of a neutral background. Again, turn to nature for inspiration. Can any accessory scheme equal the combination of buttery birch and fiery maple leaves against the background of a bright October sky? A country decorator can only try. The sumptuous variety of nature's own background colors is covered in "Walls and Wallpapers," the chapter in which you will read how to use the accessory approach to an entire house by painting the walls one unifying background color.

You can overload a home with too much color just as you can overload a room with too much furniture, and the best way to avoid the too-much look is to become increasingly discriminating. Country living tends to bring out the collector in everyone. Rarely does anyone walk in the door empty-handed, and the call of the yard sale and country auction is often too tempting to resist. With this eclectic approach to the accumulation of furnishings, who wants to worry about whether today's find will clash with tomorrow's treasure? As long as you don't overload a room with objects, if you follow the standards of quality craftsmanship and design and choose your colors and textures carefully, you can scarcely go wrong.

But be ready for surprises. Whoever would have thought that a green-painted Victorian chest would look so wonderful bearing a tole tray with its vibrant colors? Remember the old adage that nature's colors never clash; at the produce market, apples next to grapes, lemons to pumpkins, eggplant to purple cabbage never offends even the most discriminating eye. Concentrate on developing your own powers of discernment and learn to identify pure color, the kind that is infused with light and depth like a cut stone, and you won't have to worry about combinations. Will a Star-of-Bethlehem quilt look good with the bright primitive landscape of a hooked rug? If it passes nature's stringent color test, chances are the answer is yes.

The country is for touching. In the city the attitude is "Keep off" or "Please don't touch"; but in the country, tactile communion with nature is important, whether it comes from stroking a well-weathered barn door or from touching a furry mullein leaf. Unglazed clay, animal hide, bare board and bark—country textures are not limited just to the rough-hewn. Country texture is also goose down, fine old wood, buttery-soft suede, warm wool, and honest cotton.

For country dining, think candles. Here an electrified Victorian oil lamp overhead adds to the glow from white tapers set into wooden candle holders to grace the country dining table with its cover of antique quilt.

Pine walls set the background in this tack room. The worn benches were purchased from a country auction. A Currier & Ives winter scene hangs on the wall.

If your mood matches the serenity of a mother swan's glide, you may seek quiet inspiration in the arrangement—on a chopping block beside the front door—of heather asters and yellow helianthus.

Right: *Lucky are the country lady and gentleman who can enjoy an herb room lined with open shelving stocked with sage, rosemary, tarragon, oregano, camomile and violet. The soft hues of the ordinary canning jars are picked up in the Oriental rug and the handsome English yew wood chair.*

The country mailbox can be decorated to your liking. Our box is painted yellow and is decorated with birds and vines and an American flag. The box was designed and painted by our neighbor Patricia Chapman.

Glimpsed by the rural delivery mailman on his rounds: your backyard stock of wood for winter's glowing fires.

Some textures are Down Home naturals. Rich brown wide-wale corduroy is reminiscent of plowed furrows, hand-woven cloth has those wonderful nubs, and brown ultrasuede reminds one of cattails. Any texture that is reminiscent of something you love in the great out-of-doors is bound to work well indoors. Nor need your inspiration be limited to textiles. Many natural objects also shine and gleam. A glazed bowl found at a country auction may duplicate both the texture and the color of a robin's egg or a high-gloss buttercup. The not-quite-uniform look of hand-woven materials is also present in jute, burlap, and materials made of woven, twisted or braided grasses.

Is velvet an appropriate texture in a country house? There is something almost unpatriotic about lavishness in a Down Home setting—excepting, of course, for food and hospitality. To most people, country means Robert Frost's frugal New England or Willa Cather's windswept prairie farmhouse, not Monticello or Tara. Even the grace of Colonial Williamsburg is on the borderline between authentic Down Home and Country Gentry. So save your most opulent treasures for an urban setting.

A little luxury goes a long way in the country, and its scarcity makes it all the more appreciated. Many an old-time country wife sprinkled a few bits of precious velvet or satin through the design of a patchwork quilt, and because of the contrast to the calico and homespun pieces that surrounded it, the scraps of luxury were all the more valuable. But true country people don't show off, and a swath of velvet drapery at the window or superpile wall-to-wall carpeting may overpower the simple beauty of most Down Home settings.

## Line

Hardly ever are there lines in the country, even at the town bank or local supermarket. Human beings plant in rows, and roads may be laid out in straight lines, but one of the great reliefs to the weary eye of a city dweller is the country's lack of grid.

"Wildflowers, wildflowers, never in a row," goes an old song, and that kind of artless happenstance is also pleasant indoors. Apply an unregimented look to your decorating plans and avoid the uptight, four-squared, tucked-in-at-every-corner look of which so many interior designers are fond (as if neatness were a high priority in life). Order, of course, is essential, and nature is known for her orderly way of conducting business; but she's not obvious about it, and neither should you be.

Furniture shouldn't be "arranged" so much as merely put there. A couch sandwiched between two end tables, fronted by a coffee table and flanked by two matching armchairs is just too regimented a look for a country living room. Break up predictable lines. Of course, several rows of gleaming quart jars filled with fruit and vegetables, or a neat stack of Benningtonware jugs, is another matter. It's not things in lines that are to be avoided but things that look too arranged or too cluttered. Don't crowd.

**Fragrance**

A distinctive fragrance in a home is an important element of style that often gets overlooked. Heady jasmine incense may complement a room designed with mandarin opulence, and gentle tea rose may be perfect for English décor, but Down Home is made up of more zesty aromas: pine, clove pomanders, drying herbs, bayberry candles, baking apples, and of course the lingering fragrance of smoldering wood. Cherry, oak, apple, and pine—many kinds of woods have pockets of syrupy gum that give off distinctive odors. Choosing a favorite is all part of increasing your discriminating sensory powers, for in creating a style the olfactory sense is just as important as the visual, the tactile, and the auditory.

> "How gently too did the sight of the old manse . . .
> its gray homely aspect rebuke the speculative
> extravagances of the day."

Nathaniel Hawthorne describes the cumulative effect of the right colors, textures, lines, and fragrances of the overall Down Home style. Follow nature's lead and then go for the functional, choosing the most beautiful examples you can afford. What could be more satisfying than a simple Shaker bench? A basket woven of fine braided grasses? A Rose-of-Sharon starburst appliqué quilt? All these objects have a function, but it is their simple beauty that makes them so successful in a country home. A house filled with such objects, surrounded by nature's own colors, textures and fragrances, will achieve a grace beyond definition.

*Country style calls for smooth old wood—preferably pine—for the walls of your country den. For the mantel, a row of brass beehive candlesticks accompanied by a tin candle mold.*

*In the Down Home buffet setting, you're sure to find the family cat—in this case a Carissa—on the small tribal Oriental rug in front of the fire.*

Suspend a drying rack hung with rose hips from a wooden slat country ceiling.

The country look is for touching; no "Keep off" signs mar nature's treasures here. In this herb house, goldenrod and money plant grace an American pine table (circa 1850). The Pennsylvania redware on the table is another of the new collector's items.

A Sears, Roebuck stove and a plank-seat kitchen chair accentuate the special country charm of the brick floor. in this herb house. Drying rose hips hang from the wood beams.

Here, in harmony with the out-of-doors, is a charming English cottage among the trees and vines. Note the hanging broom at the door and the bird house among the greenery.

# Country Lights

"At the window winks the flickering fire light,
Here and there the lamps of evening glimmer,
   Social watchfires
Answering one another through the darkness."

Henry Wadsworth Longfellow

Technology is astonishing in some respects—and quite unsuccessful in others. Eyes can be operated on by laser beams, but ask a lighting expert to duplicate the sunlight of a late October afternoon, and he or she will probably not even come close. In the country, there is sunlight, moonlight, and starlight; inside, we do the best we can to illuminate small, intimate areas rather than whole rooms, thereby avoiding competition with those master lighting technicians, the sun and the moon.

In general, Down Home lighting should be scaled down: don't use overhead lights at all unless they are low, such as over a dining table. The typical country house is small and intimate, not grand and sweeping. Inside city rooms, every cubic inch may be lit like a piazza in the noonday sun. But the light in a country home should be soft and glimmering, each area of lighted space no larger than necessary to avoid eyestrain.

*Down Home lighting should be scaled down. A small lamp with a printed-fabric shade lights up a side chest. A wall bracket of amber glass placed low adds to the cozy atmosphere, and a tier of wall-hung candles supplements the soft light.*

"Should not every apartment in which man dwells be lofty
enough to create some obscurity overhead, where flickering
shadows may play at evening about the rafters?"

*Henry David Thoreau*

The traditional approach to country lighting was not poetic in the least
but merely practical: children needed light to study by, mother to sew by,
father to make repairs by. And each family member probably had a candle
to carry to bed, in a holder often shaped so that the thumb could be slipped
through it for safety. Candles dripped, kerosene smoked, and the danger of
fire was always present.

Fortunately for the country decorator, adhering to tradition need apply
only to the holder, not the flame. The receptacles our forebears used for
keeping the flame are many, varied, and often beautiful. They are available
in wood, glass, pewter, silver, or tin. They are plain and they are fancy. The
soothing mellow-yellow, intimate kind of light that is so desirable in the
country rules out the harshness of the high overhead light, the superwatt
bulb or the greenish-blue glare of the fluorescent tube. Of course it is possible
to achieve a Down Home mood with the incandescent light bulb, but first,
try mingling the electric light with candles.

The early settlers burned cattails, or "rush lights," in their somber homes
after the sun went down. Candlemaking was a messy and time-consuming
necessity. When they butchered, they rendered the animal fat and made
tallow candles; or they dipped wick into melted beeswax. Coastal dwellers
made fragrant bayberry candles by cooking the small, luminous gray berries
found growing near the beaches until they released their small amount of oil.
When it was discovered that spermaceti, a fat from the head of the sperm
whale, burned with twice the candlepower of beeswax or tallow, the great
whaling industry was born to supply an ever increasing number of lamps for
the growing populations of the Atlantic and Pacific seaboards. The boats
came in, the years went by, and the flickering night-lights began to spread in-
land until East met West and an entire continent was illuminated at night
with candles in holders that differed in style as widely as the kinds of people
who had settled this country.

Today it is still possible to decorate with glimmering, warm and always
flattering candlelight, as intimate a glow as that of the flare from a fireplace.
Try using groups of candles in an infinite variety of holders, sconces,
chandeliers, lanterns, and glass lamps from the age before Edison. They il-

*A country mantel calls for country things: stoneware, metal molds, and—yes—a pewter candlestick.*

luminate cozy areas with rosy yellow light and leave in mysterious shadow the surrounding unlit areas all the way to Thoreau's obscure rafters.

Candles do not afford the best light to read by, and some people claim they can't eat by them either (perhaps they should try using more of them on the table or overhead), but candlelight can't be surpassed for illuminating the conversation that takes place during those precious hours between the end of productivity and bed. Candles probably cast the most romantic light in the world (surpassed only by moonlight) to talk by, to listen to music by, and to make love by. Candlelight is always wonderful in the country.

There is something very satisfying about buying candles by the box. Storing away enough light for the long winter dark (with an homage to all those country folk before you who had to make their own laboriously by hand) is another of those strong atavistic urges that are so important to satisfy while country decorating.

Try a series of candles at different heights on the mantel or coffee table, although the latter is an all-too-familiar repository for the latest decorator cliché. Such objects are called "statements," but they usually say nothing at all: a fishbowl filled with three calla lilies, a trio of obelisks, or three fat candles. If you do put candles on your coffee table, by all means use them. Then they won't be a "statement" but a light source. Remember, if you choose objects for their usefulness rather than some kind of visual effect, your house will never look cluttered. In the country, the point is not to fill; it's to use.

Country folk before the age of the light bulb burned their candles in beautiful Bennington stoneware, mercury glass, or wood or tin chandeliers. They set them in iron or wood floorstand holders with brass fittings, some with adjustable arms for reading or for conversation. They hung them on the wall in brackets of China-trade porcelain, brass, pewter or tin, often with reflectors for increased light and safety. Put enough candle holders around—whether they sit on the floor or a table, hang on the wall or from the ceiling—to satisfy even the one who complains, "But I can't see what I'm eating!"

With all those candles around, you have a good excuse for buying another pleasurable remnant of the past—a candle snuffer. Its graceful design will add to your overall decorating concept of beauty married to function, for a snuffed candle does not leave behind a trail of unpleasant smoke, as does the candle that has been blown out.

### Lamps

The earliest lamps were little more than a dish of oil in which floated a burning rag. The American country lamp, from the primitive Betty lamp of Colonial days to the ornate Victorian lamp dripping with prisms, was for the most part merely an esthetic improvement on that age-old method. Flammable liquid, a bit of wick, and an attractive enclosure—such a lighting device will give your country home a glow of authenticity, even if you decide for safety's sake to wire it.

Gas lamps were often made of brass, decorated milk glass, or glass that was clear, ribbed or delicately etched. There were also student lamps with dark green shades in admirably simple designs, as well as wall lamps with fancy brackets. Tiffany lamps were for the wealthy, although many a country dweller had an imitation—with pieces of glass fitted into a metal frame rather than leaded together like the more expensive models of colored glass.

Outdoor lamps can also be used successfully indoors, and there are many to choose from: deck lights, railroad lanterns, miner's lamps, and the ever popular Paul Revere lantern—usually four-sided and paned with glass, but sometimes made of tin pierced with tiny holes in a pleasing pattern. In a country home a lamp with beautiful sworls of pinpricks casts interesting shadows on the wall, or sprinkles a patchwork quilt with stars of light. Although they are not adequate for reading or doing close work, they do afford a wonderfully dramatic effect.

Collectors, decorators, and other experts argue about whether antique lighting fixtures should be wired for electricity. Some wouldn't think of boring holes in a quaint little Betty lamp or a genuine Gone-with-the-Wind figured-glass fixture. Others advocate the combination of esthetics and practicality and insist that they are carrying out an American tradition in making a good thing better with modern technology. If someone wants to turn an old wood lantern from a whaling ship into a kitchen chandelier that holds three sixty-watt bulbs on a dimmer, who's to stand in judgment? As in so much of country decorating, the choice is up to you. No matter what you decide, you'll be in good company.

Before you go on an antique lighting fixture trip, it's good to remember that some of the more elegant pieces you'll see may not be appropriate to Down Home style. Heavily ornate Liberace candelabra might intimidate a simple tin sconce on a nearby wall. If you want to make a big "statement" with a light fixture, why not consider an outrageous late-Victorian piece? Wild West Bordello, Victoria Overmuch, or Great-Aunt Mildred's Hallway—whatever the connotation, these ultrafancy pieces of French gilt, cut crystal hanging in swags and fringes, and fancy glass orbs painted with roses and grapes are cherished by many with a whim for the whimsical. While some people hate Victorian excess, others are charmed by the sight of a Vaseline-yellow sandwich glass lamp in a heart-and-honeycomb design. For the latter group, it conjures up visions of gingerbread, hot cider, and a houseful of visiting cousins. Whether you use such pieces depends on what they trigger in your own sense memory. Trying to decide whether they are in good taste is really beside the point. In a house full of utilitarian objects of beauty, each carefully selected for its honest simplicity, a silly Victorian piece can be an amusing, affectionate contrast.

When the late-twentieth-century home decorator sets out to interpret the past, the present tends to get in the way. Many readers of this book will relate to Down Home concepts filtered through interior design ideas they already hold, like opening up small spaces with mirrored walls, or painting them a glossy white, so that rooms are lit up as if they were always about to have their picture taken. This widespread approach to lighting reflects the expansionist thinking of more-and-more, of better-things-through-better-living-through-chemistry, and of progress-is-our-most-important-product.

We should approach lighting the country house by shedding the present and really trying to envision that womblike atmosphere of the past. Close your eyes and try to see small areas in which light is dispersed in low candlepower, not three-way bulbs, rows of tubing or powerful overhead lights.

These interiors may be more subdued than most of us are accustomed to, but do we really need so much artificial light in our lives? A room painted sky blue or pale melon and lit with many small lamps of brass, wood or glass decked out in lampshades of a simple print or homespun check will be far more serene and relaxed than the room in which one or two huge lamps, with harsh white lampshades, flank the couch.

Lampshades often end up a joke, even when not worn on the head. Together with their bases, they represent one of the most common problems in decorating, for professionals as well as do-it-yourself people. But light fixtures can be made less of a problem by adhering to a simple rule: honor an object's past. Avoid turning something into a lamp that was once a coffee urn, a ginger jar, or a mechanical bank. The best lamp is one that was always a lamp. Whether it should be used as is or wired is an individual decision.

No honest, forthright country home needs a porcelain head of George Washington wearing a lampshade. Drums of the kind that little boys played in a bygone year are also sometimes made into lamps, with the sticks neatly crossed in front. Wine jugs, wire dress forms, wagon wheels, dolls, toy wooden horses, crackerboxes and even flowerpots are being turned into lamps or chandeliers. But it's just as effective to set a doll or ginger jar in front of a simple lamp and let the collectible be a movable factor. Jars are put to better use when they hold sweet peas or zinnias and are surrounded by fat white candles of various sizes.

Some successfully wired antique lamps are the tole fixtures with three candles and a shade, as are the many bracket lamps with tulip-shaped shades. Chandeliers were used over a dining table for so many years that many styles abound, from rugged railroad lamps to delicately fluted oil lamps with painted roses. These fixtures can contain bulbs that from below will give the look of the original light source.

Reproductions in lamps rarely evoke the honesty that is so important to a country home. While the "real thing" always has a certain character by not pretending to be what it is not, many reproductions look like charlatans, pretend objects that have been made to look old. An outsized reproduction of a milk can painted bright colors and turned into a lamp is like no milk can that ever was. It simply doesn't make sense as a lamp. All these potential mistakes can easily be avoided by buying the originals. Somewhere, perhaps in a pile of junk, your antique lamp awaits. The search for the many lighting devices that are needed to illuminate small areas with low, mellow light is one of the most satisfying tasks in Down Home decorating. The happy glow of these lights will warm the heart from both within and without the house.

*Remember the old gas lanterns? You can still find them, though many have been electrified. In the nostalgic atmosphere of this Down Home attic, an original gas lantern fixture lights up the trunks and valises of yesterday. The photograph was taken at Teddy Roosevelt's Sagamore Hill.*

*The candle is an American favorite. Here the glow of candlelight enhances a small hanging bookshelf.*

*This English settee was crafted in 1650. The oblong pewter pieces are rare, as is the lanthorn or lantern hanging on the wall. The "glass" of the lanthorn is melted cow's horn.*

*This milkglass oil lantern—an attractive version of a
centuries-old favorite—sits on a Sheraton table beside a
window curtained with popular sheer tiebacks. The graceful
wing chair is sized for the lady of the house.*

*Non-electrified oil lamps are available in antique shops around the country. I use them for party decorations for country dining tables. The oil lamp spells romance to me— especially when accompanied by a glowing fire.*

# The Country Kitchen

What is your dream of the ultimate country kitchen? A gleaming row of cabinets and empty counters, as sterile as an operating room? Hardly. The kitchen is the room in the country house that brings most vividly to mind the deepest and most satisfying of sense memories, because all the senses are employed: sight, sound, taste, touch and smell. This is the room that can fulfill your deepest longings.

Perhaps the kitchen of your dreams is a large, warm and fragrant room, big enough to seat twenty for an old-fashioned Thanksgiving but cozy enough for a fireside meal for two. Its fireplace, perhaps, is enormous, big enough for two Santas to come down.

The kitchen of most people's dreams has enough counter space for several cooks to roll out pie crusts, dress a pheasant, and cut vegetables for a stir-fry—all at the same time. There's also a big refrigerator, a hefty freezer, a

*People are moving back to the kitchen that is reminiscent of the old-fashioned keeping room.*

six-burner stove, a double sink, and all the conveniences a good cook cannot live without. The big dining table is wood—round or oval, or of wide planks. The chairs are comfortable enough for extended after-feast conversation.

Around the fireplace there's a rocking chair, a lamp with enough light to read or sew by, a few more comfortable chairs, and a hooked rug in primitive colors. Perhaps there's even room for a simple pine desk and a glassed-in breakfront for a treasured collection of fly patterns.

People tend to congregate in your dream kitchen. The room is warm and fragrant, the atmosphere friendly and inviting. When people want to be alone they retire to another part of the house, but when they want to linger, there always seems to be someone in the kitchen to linger with.

If this description of a dream kitchen sounds vaguely familiar, it could be that we all dream the same dream when we reflect on what really makes us happy. And happier still will be the Down Home decorator who, after re-creating the best of the past—the lure of the keeping room of our ancestors—makes it even more desirable with modern conveniences.

It's not so strange to yearn for what we had before the advent of the "efficiency kitchen," and nowhere are those yearnings stronger than in the country. The separation of the kitchen from the rest of the house isn't as recent an idea as the efficiency kitchen, however. Mid-nineteenth-century Henry David Thoreau was already severely objecting to the proliferation of the dining room:

> "Nowadays the host does not admit you to *his* hearth,
> but has got the mason to build one for yourself somewhere
> in his alley, and hospitality is the art of *keeping* you
> at the greatest distance. There is as much secrecy
> about the cooking as if he had a design to poison you."

As the population became more affluent, cultured people simply did not entertain guests in the kitchen. The kitchen was now a place where food was prepared and the dishes were washed and little more. Then it became smaller and smaller. By the middle of the twentieth century the nuclear family had shrunk, and the kitchen was just big enough for mom; the rest of the family activity was scattered about the house. No room really replaced the cozy keeping room. The living room was still reserved for company, the dining room was just a room to eat in, and the family recreation room was too noisy ever to be cozy. Retreating to the bedroom was another alternative, but that was isolating. It seemed people didn't really congregate anymore except to eat a hurried meal.

Meanwhile, in the kitchen, mom was experiencing some severe isolation herself. For the first time, perhaps, in the history of the human race, a lone woman was put in charge of feeding an entire family. This she did in a spotless, gleaming room that was supposed to be kept so tidy that it didn't look as if any cooking went on in it. Everything was tucked away in rows of cupboards; anything left out on the counter was given a modest little cover. It was a kind of Buck Rogers hurtling-through-the-space-age kitchen—streamlined, gadgeted, and somehow chilling with its cold stainless steel and Formica. In the efficiency kitchen, clutter somehow connoted uncleanliness.

Fortunately, a new trend is upon us. As nuclear families break up, remarry, and generally form new ties, people are living as extended families again. Consequently, the dream of a kitchen that is reminiscent of the old keeping room is not just a dream at all; it's a practical idea! All over the country—especially *in* the country—people are moving back to the kitchen, knocking down walls to do so if they must. Fortunately many of those walls separating the kitchen from the dining room are not supporting walls, and removal is not a major renovation job.

The custom of more than one working cook in the kitchen is a good one, although a country kitchen should be big for another reason: it's a far more serious place than a city kitchen. The urge to stock up is great in the country. Little homesteads may be far away from a store, and it's difficult to ignore the strong instinct that urges us to imitate the animals and store up food for lean times. Besides, stocking up makes economic sense, especially if you have a productive garden.

Food reserves call for storage space: a pantry, a root cellar, lots of shelving. The satisfaction of seeing them filled will be worth the effort of installing them. Buying or harvesting in bulk may also require room for bins, canning equipment, and jars for herbs and dried mushrooms.

For all these and many more reasons, the kitchen of one's dreams tends to be large. But large is not enough, even if filled with Hepplewhite, genuine Early American pine, a slate floor, a Garland stove, and matching Windsor rockers around the massive brick fireplace. Even in such a kitchen, if no one likes to cook, the mood of the room will not be the "real thing" but a reproduction.

Some people, feeling it's time for a change in their country house, hire a decorator and say, "Give me a really strong country look in this kitchen."

The decorator knows how to satisfy their desires for that kind of "look"—and installs a set of ribbed American glass jars filled with pasta, black beans, dried peppers and wheat berries. He or she hangs a yard of oregano and braided onion from an exposed beam overhead, along with a collection of baskets and antique tinware. Shelves are filled with treen and Benningtonware jugs. Pennsylvania Dutch noodle boards and a set of fancy Victorian cooky cutters hang on the wall.

Year after year these objects sit or hang, gathering dust, which is dutifully removed by the hired cleaning help. An individual hired to come in to cook or clean is rarely sufficiently interested to create a room that really looks as if it's used and enjoyed, and the non-cooking couple who requested a real Down Home look in their kitchen find that all they really have is a replication of a kitchen.

Now for the good news: if you *do* like to cook, or love to eat and want to do more cooking in the country, your kitchen decorating project can't miss. In fact, the more you like to cook, the more inviting your new kitchen will be.

Start your dream kitchen by thinking about the floor. A kitchen floor should first of all be easy to clean. Aside from all the regular in-and-out traffic, the country kitchen floor gets dirty from flour spilled by overexuberant dough kneaders; other similar messes occur with "start from scratch" cooking. Although cleanliness is a primary consideration, memory is another. The oldest memories are of tamped earth, then stone, then wood, and, only recently, synthetic floor coverings. A stone floor seems to be the most popular choice in a dream kitchen, followed by wood. With the new heavy-duty varnishes, a wood kitchen floor is now also practical. It's also easier on the feet, and it gives falling dishes a fighting chance.

Both wood and stone make ideal borders for small handcrafted rugs—hooked, woven, or crocheted. Another touch of authenticity comes with painting an old wood floor, using earth colors and giving it several coats of varnish. You may also want to consider stenciling your newly painted floor. (See the "Country Floors" chapter for more ideas.)

Once the dimensions and the flooring have been determined, plan your work space. First picture in your mind the maximum use you want from your dream kitchen. Then make the necessary economic adjustments, and plan for the maximum.

A communal kitchen means room enough for several people to work in as well as space to move back and forth. An island counter around which many can have fun is one good solution, as are L- or U-shaped counters. Don't

A country kitchen should have lots of shelves. Mrs. Lawson
Hamilton of Lewisburg, West Virginia, has used hers to display a collection of salt-glaze pottery.

scrimp on counter space. Nothing is so frustrating as a kitchen with insufficient worktop space.

After you have envisioned a likely cast of characters all happily at it in the kitchen, consider a few more feet for the person who suddenly has an irresistible yen to make her aunt's apple strudel or his own original eggplant lasagna. People tend to get involved in a country kitchen. Indulge them if you can with a little more counter space. Even those who say they have no interest in cooking will be drawn into the food preparation by the sight of tomatoes they can actually peel and the milky aroma of freshly picked corn. Most houseguests really don't want to be kept out of the kitchen, and why should they be, when it's such an inviting place?

Once you have made room for a maximum number of cooks, it's time to get down to the cooking. The best country kitchen is the one that is planned after careful consultation with one's recipe collection. For, as you are what you eat, your kitchen should be what you cook. For the readers who think cooking is either beyond or beneath them, read on. You might change your mind.

What kind of cook are you? Is your specialty pastry? Then you will need a special kind of country kitchen in which you can fulfill a yearning to try puff pastry or make all your own pasta and bread. The finest pasta shop in the world won't sell you a product made from organically grown spinach picked that morning, and the fanciest bread store won't carry a graham loaf that's still a little too warm to cut.

There are other considerations for the serious baker: bins for graham, rye, whole wheat, and other flours; a marble slab for kneading; and storage containers to keep big batches of baked goods fresh (although they never last that long).

The tables of other country households, particularly those in mountain, lake or river country, may feature a lot of fish and game. Provide for messy jobs like filleting fish or dressing pheasants in your kitchen. And don't forget a good chopping block and a place for a meat grinder or a pasta machine if your recipes call out for a homemade ingredient. Canning is another consideration, as anyone will attest who has tried to sterilize quart jars in a small kitchen.

In other words, prepare for plenty. That doesn't mean you're doomed to gain weight in the country. To the contrary, the low-calorie cook will also need lots of space to prepare vegetables Japanese-style for crisp-tender cooking. There are also those excellent *nouvelle cuisine* meat and vegetable stocks so necessary to low-carbohydrate cooking.

Another thing about country food preparation is the great satisfaction gained from the sheer quantity that one can prepare. Less food is wasted in the country than in the city, where space is at a premium. Leftovers can simmer in a soup pot for a day or two, stone soup style, until a nourishing and delicious soup or concentrated stock can be eaten, canned, or frozen for later use.

With cooks and menus in mind, it's time to get down to basics. Given the dimensions of your room, the location of doors and windows, how do you provide for all those dreams?

### Equipment and Appliances

First things first: where to place the sink, the stove and the refrigerator? A sink can be single or double bowl, made of porcelain or stainless steel, with one faucet or two. If you've been cooking for any length of time, you know your preferences. Unless you want to preserve the charm of the ancient sink that came with the house, you will probably be faced with the decision of what you would really rather have. Most people will opt for a two-bowl sink, especially in an active kitchen, and a single faucet that mingles hot and cold.

Sinks are best located near a window from which you can watch the scenery. A stove may also be locked into an area by the need to be near a ventilation outlet. A country stove should have a minimum of four burners, with two ovens for optimum convenience, perhaps one above and one underneath the burners. Plan for the future if your dream is going to come true in installments. Make sure the stove has ample room for big pots if you want the oven directly above it. One popular stove is the range top that can be built right into a counter. A good arrangement for avoiding too many cooks crowding around the stew is to make that counter approachable from two directions. If you are fortunate enough to have a restaurant stove or an antique appliance with built-in wells and griddles, such a stove deserves to have a kitchen planned around it.

A refrigerator should be placed in an area of the kitchen where the door can swing open easily. Refrigerators are available with hinges on either side so that the door can swing open in the desired direction. A refrigerator in the country may need to be big enough to hold garden produce, some tempting leftovers, and a few gallons of spring water, plus the usual things a refrigerator must hold. Don't scrimp on size.

Small appliances in a country home can be a problem unless you can afford to duplicate everything you have in the city. To simplify matters, you may conclude that although the country is the place for heart-shaped waffles and espresso, you can skip the former and visit a coffeehouse for the latter in the city. Small appliances will tend to accumulate, however, after your third or fourth country auction or yard sale.

What about a washer and drier? Because the kitchen is used so much and these appliances make a lot of noise, you might consider moving the laundry equipment to another room. Many country houses have built-on sheds or pantries that would suit. Even an all-purpose room can be overloaded with activity, so if there is appropriate space elsewhere, relegate washing and drying clothes to a less frequented place.

Next, you need counter space with cabinets and shelving above and below. Try marking off counter areas in your kitchen. See how a U-shaped counter would work, or a free-standing counter in the middle of the room. The most workable counter space is the continuous one that can be wiped clean in one long swish and has a generous backboard to accommodate spillage.

The standard height of a countertop is 36 inches and the standard depth 25. If you're taller or shorter than average, make adjustments. This is your kitchen, and you may not be "standard." Allow enough clearance for opening drawers and cabinet doors, and make sure your cabinets are cantilevered; that is, that the top extends a few inches out from the cabinets so you can stand close to your work.

The Down Home kitchen is really not the place for Formica. Nor is the cost of a natural material necessarily out of the question. Spend some time attending auctions and sales. Watch for notices in the paper of sales of commercial equipment. You might find the perfect butcher block or piece of marble for your kitchen counter. Another popular surface is ceramic tile, whether in unglazed terra cotta or glazed blocks. You might even find a narrow table that perfectly suits one area of your work space. Plan for the unexpected, and don't be in a hurry to buy a custom-made, order-by-number kitchen.

As for hanging cupboards, gone are the days when food was considered to be an embarrassment, to be hidden behind closed doors. Now it's out in the open again. The country collector will have shelves for an ample selection of attractive glass, wood or metal containers for storing kitchen staples. Perhaps you are fortunate enough to have old-fashioned kitchen cupboards with windowpane doors that have been painted over so many times they no longer look like glass. Why not restore them? Chances are there is some at-

*The country kitchen of everybody's dream is warm and fragrant and large, yet cozy enough for a fireside meal for two. And after the meal, hearthside is the perfect spot for reading and for enjoying the most peaceful time of the day.*

tractive wood underneath. This is one paint-removing job that's not so impossible, because the cupboard doors can be unscrewed from their hinges and worked on outside. The results will be worth the messy task—a cupboard behind which you can display your best kitchenware, free from dust and grease.

Another storage piece is the old-fashioned country cupboard. The corner ones are excellent space-savers, if you are able to include one in your early plans. Other ideas are pie safes, plain and fancy Pennsylvania German cupboards, dry sinks, or simple wall-to-wall shelving fronted with wooden shutters that may be found at an auction. Provide for plenty and you won't be sorry later.

You may be fortunate enough to have in your house a pantry, a room that easily lends itself to decorating possibilities. The typical pantry is a room off the kitchen. It may be located between the kitchen and the back porch, or it may be an extension of the original house. In times past the pantry was kept colder than the rest of the house, but not so cold that jars of canned goods would freeze and burst. The pantry was also the place where people shook off snow, removed overshoes, and prepared themselves for the blast of fragrant warm air from the kitchen.

The pantry remains a potential multipurpose room that should be given emphasis in your renovating plans. It's a good place to store ski gear, or to perform messy jobs like potting plants or cleaning fish. You can also use it for a dry cellar, taking advantage of its cooler temperature for storing food reserves through the winter. Installed with a windowed roof, it can be turned into a greenhouse in which flowering plants can be grown for a little exotic side show during the worst of winter's icy blasts. Used thus, it is also a place to start seedlings for the big garden; here they may be kept under commercial growing lights to give them that important head start.

As a handy transitional room, your pantry may need no more decoration than a paint job, shelving, and rows of mason jars. The country is the place to turn your dreams into reality, and your inspiration may be in as humble a place as a pantry. Let it fly. You might find that the pantry adapts itself perfectly to your particular interests and life-style.

The country dweller who is fortunate enough to afford a fireplace in the kitchen will need to include it in the original house plans. A fireplace will always manage to become the focal point of any room, but it's especially true of a dining area in the kitchen. Provide for it with rockers, armchairs, or benches for the many pastimes that go on in the kitchen between meals. Turn to "Country Fireplaces" for some additional inspiration.

For optimum kitchen light, the windows should offer multiple exposure. Perhaps the most important window in your house is the one above the sink, because you spend more time looking out of it than any other. Leave it bare to expose the maximum view. Shutters or curtains (chosen with care to complement the Down Home requirements of natural color and small, modest country prints) should be installed so they can shut out the night but also be pulled back to bring in the outside as the sun moves around the house. Lighting a kitchen well is important, as the room is used day and night for many purposes. Rather than one harsh overhead light, use a number of smaller lamps. (See "Country Lights" for some decorating ideas.) A table also used for homework, crafts, needlework or conversation will need one or several light sources, as will comfortable chairs for reading. Overhead lights should be kept low. The object is never to flood a country room with needless light. Put lights on dimmers, especially overhead ones.

Once you have everything in place in your diagram of your dream kitchen, you may discover that some important items have been left out. Where is the bookcase for your ever growing cookbook collection? To say nothing of seed catalogs, wildflower- and mushroom-picking guides, record-keeping books, antiques collectors guides?

And where will you put your collection of antique pastry gadgets you love to look at as well as use for special occasions? And a big crock for making apple cider vinegar or homemade sauerkraut? All these passions and many more must be considered while making your plans—not later.

In the end, you will know whether you have managed to recapture the attraction of the old-fashioned keeping room by the number of people who tend to gravitate toward it. You'll also know how successful it is to cook in after you've prepared your first major feast. The chief advantage of a well-planned kitchen is that you can perform the space-consuming tasks in advance. Then minor surprises can be adjusted for. An up-to-date, efficient, old-fashioned country kitchen is really having your cake (or nutmeg doughnuts, or wild raspberry tarts) and eating it too: the best of the past and the present in one irresistible room. From a decorating standpoint, the well-thought-out Down Home kitchen can't fail. There is not a single fragrance, a single laugh or contented sigh emanating from such a room that could ever be judged in poor taste—except, of course, by someone who has lost his appetite for living.

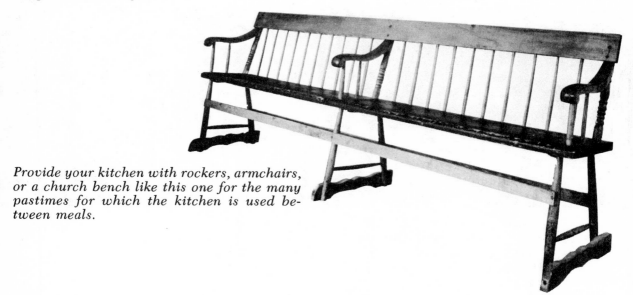

*Provide your kitchen with rockers, armchairs, or a church bench like this one for the many pastimes for which the kitchen is used between meals.*

In a good country kitchen there should be enough counter space for several cooks—to roll out pie crusts, dress a pheasant, and cut vegetables for a stir-fry, all at the same time.

Hang antique kitchen utensils beside the fireplace or on the walls of the country kitchen.

Start with an easy-to-clean floor when you plan your country kitchen. Stone is the most popular Down Home choice.

# The Gourmet Kitchen Garden

"The copperfaces, the red men, handed us . . .
The bah-tah-to, the potato, the spud.
Sunflowers came from Peruvians in ponchos,
Early Italians taught us of chestnuts,
Walnuts and peaches being Persian mementoes,
Siberians finding for us what rye might do,
Hindus coming through with the cucumber,
Egyptians giving us the onion, the pea,
Arabians handing advice with one gift:
'Some like it, some say it's just spinach.' "

*Carl Sandburg*
*The People, Yes*

Since the first colonists encountered the "bah-tah-to" and other unfamiliar New World foods, we Americans have proved to be most adventurous in expanding our repertoire of favorite dishes. The old-fashioned country garden of the past might have included some exotic varieties of food like snow peas or interesting herbs exchanged among neighbors, but our forebears, even the most adventurous of cooks and eaters, simply didn't have access to such items as winter lettuce from France, finger-sized carrots from the Netherlands, or Chinese cabbages and shungiku from the Orient. Today's Down Home gardener has the world's vegetable menu to choose from, the selection of which is a great part of the joy of country gardening.

Those tempting seed catalogs start arriving in January and February, and the colorful pictures of Big Boy tomatoes and Argentine marrow squash, purple-podded Royalty green beans and tiny, glossy French aubergines send

*For the Down-Homer with a bent for collecting, here's an idea: Bring home breads from France, Holland, Belgium — wherever you travel. Display them dried on kitchen shelves, and hang hops (for making beer) above.*

country gardeners into reveries of the best crops ever . . .

Many down-to-earth factors must be considered, however, before you can give substance to dreams. Gardening is like raising children, in that when your rows of vegetables need attention, they need it *now*. If snow is in the air, for instance, and your seedlings are less than two inches high, you will have to attend to them, no matter what.

First things first: you must give your vegetables the best growing conditions possible. No matter where you live, the soil in your garden will be a good growing medium for some things but not for others. Vegetables are a quirky lot and have a variety of preferences. Take advantage of the services offered by the local agricultural extension in your community to learn about them. These experts will be able to test your soil and to advise you about different soil preparations and about growing organically.

The amount of time and money you are willing to put into soil preparation will have a lot to do with your garden's success. Scrimpers and step-skippers will usually be sorry sometime during the growing season. The secret of a vegetable garden is to grow things fast. You want to give your seedlings every advantage: the best soil medium, high in organic content and also friable—loose enough so that tender vegetable roots don't have to push themselves through the soil. The carrot that has to work hard is going to be tougher than the little-finger-sized beauty grown in well-worked soil. Get down on your hands and knees and really feel what you're working with: you'll find that the aroma and texture of well-prepared soil is a satisfaction in itself.

When your soil is ready, it's time to decide how to lay out the garden. It doesn't have to be the traditional rectangular shape with everything all in a row. You may want to put some of that rich earth into containers. They allow for more controlled gardening conditions, all the while they look wonderful from a decorative standpoint. A garden can also be terraced—a good layout, by the way, for anyone subject to back pain. Crops can be grown in big wooden tubs or pottery jars or boxes which can be elevated with borders of heavy railroad ties or stones. They can be set into L-shaped containers in corners, or hung in pots on the wall.

Containers can be covered with cloth or glass, to extend the growing season at both ends. The smaller ones can also be moved around as the sun journeys through summer. When the pea vines, for instance, start to turn dry, they can be pulled out and a new crop started, one that loves nitrogen-enriched soil. Other containers can be prepared with custom-made mixtures for plants that like lots or little acid, high or low nitrogen, lots or very little water, lots of sand or lots of peat moss or manure that has aged until all the seeds in it have sprouted. From a botanical as well as a design standpoint, the container garden is the total winner.

What to grow? The seed catalogs will dazzle you as you sit at the kitchen table in the middle of winter. Some choices may be made on the basis of appearance. Is it an extravagant waste of garden space to have two rows of corn, just for the look? Should you try both red and gold tomatoes this year? How about a row of Italian broad beans? Asparagus? Formidable, but worth a look . . .

Why not skip the ever prolific zucchini this year and try some tender little avacodella squash instead? The best-laid garden plans, like those for the country kitchen, are made around a cook's repertoire and spirit of adventure. For the enthusiastic cook, the country garden offers two kinds of fare. One is simplicity itself: new potatoes gently scrubbed and cooked in their jackets with fresh dill. Or tiny carrots steamed with fresh mint. Some things in the garden are too delicious to eat any way but straight-and-simple, as anyone who has eaten Swiss chard steamed or in a salad will attest.

The other kind of successful country cooking is international cuisine, possible because you're home-growing those expensive and hard-to-find ingredients—including some of the "optionals" you never could find! From a raw vegetable platter with a chumas dip to your finest Buddha's Delight, the gourmet garden will enhance any dish.

The country gardener's blessings are too many to count: better health, for one, from exercise in the open air. And improved health also from eating fresh produce free of chemicals. Top-quality produce is another blessing—vegetables better tasting than you could imagine. Money saved is another advantage. With food prices rising so rapidly, your savings will increase to a point in the not-too-distant future when having a plot of land and not growing food will be sheer foolishness. With all these important advantages, it's hard to understand why anyone wouldn't want to have a country garden.

After you have made your selections and ordered your seeds and bulbs for the exotica, you will want to learn everything you can in the intervening months about growing your chosen vegetables and fruits. Consider cold frames started a month or two early, using seeds rather than nursery plants. That way you can have a much larger selection. For instance, the onion: why not grow garlic and shallots as well? And how about silverskin or red onions? Why not try your hand at leeks? They must be blanched during growth by banking with sand (as with celery, sunlight makes them tough), which is why leeks are always so difficult to clean. The prolific onion, particularly the more expensive gourmet varieties, will also make good gifts—braided with a selection of garlic and shallots, the white and purple varieties.

As for the plain and simple, what is comparable in taste to the ordinary carrot fresh from the garden? An abundance of carrots will be especially appreciated by fresh vegetable juice lovers. A concoction made from carrots, celery, beets and parsley is a welcome rejuvenator to a guest arriving wilted from the city.

For some, plain mashed turnips awaken fond memories of past country meals; for others it's the rich meaty texture of acorn squash that's evocative. Green beans are good enough to eat straight from the stem, and it's a temptation when shelling peas to eat them straight from the pod because they're so delicious. Why not try growing snow peas? Most people have only known the frozen variety. The crunch of a sweet garden snow pea pod is too memorable an experience to miss.

A commercially grown green pepper has a commercially perfected hard skin to make that vegetable more transportable. Home-grown peppers seem to have no skin at all, only juice. Try roasting them with pimentoes. Greens are another common pleasure, from the first soft looseleaf lettuce to crinkled thick spinach leaves to the glorious heads of bibb and *Chicorées frisées*. All are superior to standard salad fare at the city supermarket.

But it is the old-fashioned tomato that bears the least resemblance to its commercial counterpart. The plastic container of three or four hard pink-to-orange rocks you buy in the supermarket are as pathetic an excuse for a tomato as a canned green bean in comparison to the fresh kind. The country tomato is a fruit so succulent, so heavy with richness, that it would never make it to market in one piece. A variety of hybrids is available to the home gardener. Some make excellent sauce. Others are meant to be eaten, salt shaker in hand, directly from the plant. Then there are yellow, nonacidic tomatoes for those who cannot tolerate the red ones.

Other temptations: celery, winter salad greens, gingerroot, pumpkins. . . . But don't forget: vegetables are demanding. Each kind will require a little coddling: you will be pruning and pinching, pulling weeds, picking off bugs, rescuing plants from wind and flood. Don't take on more than you can take care of. Start small and then expand.

No country kitchen is complete without a well-stocked herb garden—all the familiar English basics as well as some representatives from around the globe. It's hard to believe that the tomato didn't meet basil until the discovery of the New World, but the East-West combination has remained one of the most successful. Other herbs that enhance the tomato are oregano, dill, and summer savory. For those who have never been able to find fresh coriander for Mexican and Oriental dishes, why not try growing it? Coriander is the seed of the Chinese parsley, but the fresh coriander of Oriental and Mexican cooking comes from the leaves. Dill is another must, especially for cucumber growers. Homemade garlic dill pickles should have lots of feathery dill leaves as well as seed stuffed into their jars. Dill is beautiful to look at as well as tasty sprinkled in a summer salad.

Some herbs are not so graceful as dill or so bushy as a well-pinched basil plant; they are loved for their aromatic qualities, not their looks. Tarragon is a popular one. Dropped into a bottle of good wine vinegar, it is the essential ingredient in many an artful salad dressing.

Herbs should not be left around drying for ornamental purposes. Hanging from the rafters, they will quickly gather dust and cooking grease. So put them into tightly covered jars and store in a cool place as soon as they have released all their moisture.

How about growing all the ingredients for a superior tomato sauce? Here is a recipe that combines no fewer than five ingredients from a typical kitchen garden. It is a classic tomato sauce with a hundred different uses. There are three reasons why the recipe will appeal to many cooks: first, a true pasta lover is never satisfied with a store-bought sauce. Second, many tomato aficionados would never buy a tomato in a can. And third, cooking up a batch of tomato sauce can be a messy, time-consuming business. In this recipe, fresh tomatoes, celery, herbs, onions, and garlic simmer until the flavor is full-bodied. Then the mixture is strained through a colander. It can be put up in pint or quart jars, following the stringent rules for canning. Or it can be frozen as ice cubes and stored in your freezer. Here is Edna Revland's tomato sauce recipe:

To a six-quart porcelain pot (do not use aluminum or cast iron) add enough ripe, ripe tomatoes chopped up into quarters (it's not necessary to peel them, since they will be pressed through a colander) to fill the pot five-sixths full. Add five ribs of celery, finely chopped; a big handful of chopped parsley; a clove of garlic, chopped; two very large onions, chopped fine; and another big handful of fresh sweet basil cut from the garden as the tomatoes start to simmer. Also add two store-bought bay leaves. Simmer very slowly until the celery is soft, then force through a food mill or colander. Return to kettle and season to taste. The seasoning is an extremely individual matter. A rough estimate is: 3 or 4 teaspoons of salt, ¼ cup of lemon juice, a tablespoon of Worcestershire sauce, and a dash of Tabasco. Some cooks add a teaspoon of sugar. Again, it's a matter of taste, and the tasting is sheer pleasure. Yield: approximately six quarts.

You can follow the canning method outlined in any good cookbook, but one of the best publications is the bulletin on canning put out by the U. S. Department of Agriculture. If you want to freeze the sauce into cubes, fill six to eight ice cube trays at a time and leave them overnight in the coldest part of your freezer. (Cover, or your entire freezer will exude garlic.) The next day, pop the cubes into plastic bags. The ziplock ones are ideal. The cubes can be dropped handily into hot bouillon or ratatouille; into meat drippings for a rich gravy; or into a pot of baked beans or a hearty stew or soup; or they can be thawed in quantity for a pasta sauce.

In this age of stir-fried vegetables and *nouvelle cuisine*, few canned vegetables, even the home-canned ones, are really palatable. Because of the need to boil at high temperatures, beans, peas, and other tender vegetables become overcooked during the canning method. But pickling and preserving are most rewarding. The best pickle is one that was picked the morning it was stuffed into a jar, crisp enough to break in half. Most commercial jams and jellies can't hold a candle to homemade preserves. (The health-conscious cook can substitute honey for refined sugar and reduce the amount whenever possible.)

Canning became an art because it was a necessity; now we can use canning methods more discriminately, and freeze those vegetables we don't want to eat any way but crisp. A home freezer is a necessary part of your kitchen if you are an inveterate vegetable grower. Although anything that is to be frozen must first be blanched to stop enzyme action, the vegetable frozen straight from the garden manages to maintain much of its flavor and crunchiness. Only the fussiest purist could object to home-frozen produce, particularly in the middle of winter.

But man does not live by vegetables alone. After your garden has expanded and begun to thrive, you may want to get into wine. And why *not* grow some grapes? A grape arbor over a deck or patio is a delight both to look at and to sit under. A wine maker may want to experiment with a Pinot Noir or a Riesling grape. (A jam maker will also want to lay claim to the vines.) The gourmet root cellar can be turned into a wine cellar.

Or perhaps you'd like to venture into mushrooms. The root cellar can also become a growing medium for common champignons, dark, musky Japanese mushrooms, or wild *Boletus edulis* edibles. Commercial growers will sell entire mushroom-growing kits. If and when you become inundated with mushrooms, try drying them. They too make an excellent gift for a serious cook.

On to dessert. Wild fruits and berries may grow all around your country home, but it's also nice to try domesticating some. Although you will lose a good portion of your crop to the birds, no gourmet's garden is complete without a little fruit grown for dessert to go with some tangy cheese. Don't forget to include a clump of rhubarb, a guaranteed nostalgia item. Strawberry-rhubarb pie is a great favorite among people who remember bygone years, and both fruits can be grown with great success—the rhubarb like a weed, and the strawberries with a little T.L.C.

> " 'How are the crops this year?'
> 'Not so good for a good year,
> but not so bad for a bad year.' "
>
> *Carl Sandburg*
> The People, Yes

*Big kitchen crocks are great for making apple cider vinegar or sauerkraut. And they are great for giving your kitchen the Down Home look.*

An herb garden takes the center spot in this kitchen at Sleepy Hollow. Various potted herbs sit on the counter in the bay window. Rush-seat ladder-back chairs are used around the antique pine table.

The country collector does not hide his treasures behind closed doors. This Down Homer is proud to share the beauty of his collection of basketry, wooden bowls and pewter.

Myrtle growing in a natural clay pot enjoys the out-of-doors in the summertime. When winter arrives, the pot can be moved inside for decorative as well as spicy appeal.

# Ragbag Art

How totally American is the piecework quilt, and how quintessentially Down Home. The finest examples of this form of textile art are already national treasures, hung on many a museum and gallery wall to be admired. Like everything authentically American, patchwork has become chic in the last decade or so. But no matter where it is encountered, even when it's surrounded by latex and polyethylene, the charm of patchwork—the honesty and purity of its design—is a symbol of that rare and wonderful combination of thrift and art.

Patchwork works well practically anywhere: on the bed, the table, other furniture, and even the wall; and surely nowhere on earth does it shine in all its joyous colors as it does in a Down Home environment. A rural home without a patchwork quilt is like a farmhouse without a kitchen—unthinkable!

*American quilts are material treasures. The honesty and purity of their designs shine both in the modern home and in the Down Home environment. This is from the permanent collection of New York's Whitney Museum.*

American history itself was written in patchwork, pieced and stitched together by hand; and often a family history was stitched into it as well. But the piecework quilt did not originate in the New World. It is probably as old as poverty, as needle and thread; for centuries people have stitched together bits of cloth to keep warm under at night.

The old chant about some in rags, some in tags, and one in a velvet gown is an accurate description of what many a patchwork quilt was made of. Many times the result was a helter-skelter ragtag art with a bit of velvet elegance stitched throughout. The piecework quilt came to this country on the *Mayflower*, since its passengers were required to bring their own bedding, but its ancestry is hard to trace. A quilt was used until it was worn, then stitched to another top to become backing; then perhaps cut up and made into something else useful before being discarded. A quilt was considered a necessity; only recently has it become an heirloom.

The earliest American quilts are now museum pieces, and they are really not so pleasing in a country home as the later versions, because there is something a bit too lavish and European about them. Often the early Colonial quilt was made from a whole piece of fabric—an ornate chintz imported from India, perhaps, stitched to a border on all four sides. It was a showy piece, and not particularly creative in that the quilting simply followed the outline of the printed design. Of course the owner of such a quilt was fairly well off, because a piece of whole cloth was costly in those days, and it was sure to have been imported if the cloth was printed.

For most early Americans, a bedcover consisted of bits of cloth stitched together and quilted to a homespun backing. Somewhere, in someone's frugal keeping room, the American patchwork quilt was born. More likely it was born simultaneously in many homes; much folk art originated in this way—out of both necessity and a love of beauty.

With an ear to the winter wind rattling the windowpanes, the country wife of another age settled down for an evening of relaxation after a day of grueling toil to have a little fun planning her next quilt. Opening her ragbag, she pulled out a sky-blue church dress too small for any of her growing daughters to wear. A faded and worn visiting dress came next, violets sprinkled over dark green homespun. Then a pair of brown twill Sunday trousers, worn beyond repair. For the mandatory touch of red, there was a worn velvet weskit big enough to allow one crimson square per block, just enough fabric to brighten the overall design.

A dark accent was now needed to complement all the faded pieces. Out came the out-of-fashion widow's weeds of black wool. Hoping there would be no further need for the gown, our country wife decided to cut it up to round out her design. Wishing for a bit of bright green or pink or even a rich brown, the country wife thought out her plan. A forgotten bit of luxury came to mind: a gold satin buskin ripped down the back, a hand-me-down from a rich relative. The quilt maker returned it to her ragbag; there was quite enough luxury with the bit of red, and the next quilt would need that bit of gold satin.

Through many long winter evenings, the country wife cut and sewed until her eyes ached as she created a historical collage of weddings, funerals, births and other rites of passage. When her quilt was finished, she started another. Quilt making was a continuing activity, because as many as four or five quilts were used on each bed.

A hundred years later, you, the country decorator, marvel at the quilt with the bits of red velvet scattered through its design. "Think of the time that went into this," you say. True, but the quilt maker wasn't counting the hours. Most likely she saw her piecework as one of the few ways she could exercise her creativity and make something to beautify her drab surroundings. Quilting probably saved many a woman's sanity during the long, cold, dark winters, warming the maker as well as the user.

The patchwork quilt can be a marvel of geometrics, a dizzying optic. Not every quilt from this or any other era is a work of art, of course; but many have good colors and interesting designs. When you find one that appeals to you, buy it even it it's a little frayed in spots. In the great tradition of ragbag art, it can be cut up to use as something else entirely: upholstery, pillows, or a skirt to cover a small table. The old adage "Waste not, want not" is in revival in this age of depleting resources, and patchwork exemplifies the best of that ethic.

Another popular form of piecework is appliqué. If the country wife was particularly clever at turning a curved seam, or if she had an abundance of one or more colors, she might work a quilt in appliqué rather than patchwork. The finest quilts in the house were likely to be this more lavish form of piecework, which entailed cutting out shapes and stitching them to a block, turning under the edges with infinitesimal stitches. Padding was sometimes inserted between the stitches for a raised effect. A wedding quilt might have been a series of circles intertwined with hearts and flowers, to symbolize the marriage bond. To make an appliqué quilt, a country stitcher had to have enough fabric for roses, leaves, wedding rings, or whatever in the colors and prints her design called for. Because of these limitations, the appliqué quilt might be reserved for such special use as a dowry chest. Many a bride had at least a dozen fine quilts, the most precious being the appliqué piecework she brought to her marriage bed.

But the truly Down Home quilt has always been patchwork. Throughout the high latitudes, from New England to the Oregon Territory, beds were heaped high with them. America was a new country rich in resources and blessed by cheap labor, but like most developing nations it was poor in technology for a long time. Cloth was an import for much of our early history, particularly printed cloth, and like all imports it was treated by frugal rural people as though it were gold. Even after the Revolutionary War, Americans were still sending their cotton crops to England to be made into cloth and then sold back to the fledgling democracy at high prices. Not a scrap of such a precious commodity could they afford to waste. Some intricate quilts were made from as many as 14,000 pieces of scrap. Imagine the number of stitches! A quilt maker was likely to boast, and justly, about how many spools of thread had gone into her creation.

The earliest American quilts utilized whatever combination of cloth was available; among them was linsey-woolsey made of linen or cotton and wool. These mostly solid color quilts were often hand-dyed at home and sewn with decorative stitches. The plainer the quilt, the more ornate the stitchery was likely to be, as if the quilt maker felt obliged to provide fancy needlework to compensate for the drabness of the fabric. These early quilts, made before the nineteenth century, are now very rare. Many of the quilts from the last century are also rather plain, however; of solid color but with extraordinarily detailed stitching. These latter-day quilts are more recent examples of poverty's art.

The more affluent quilter was able to plan and execute a variety of patterns. The most popular method was to construct the quilt block by block, each a square containing twelve or multiples of twelve stitched-together patches. The block might constitute a pattern by itself, or it might become part of a larger pattern when joined with other blocks. Some of the most extraordinary quilts of this era are the pattern-within-a-pattern geometrics. To the contemporary eye, the most pleasing designs are likely to be those of rural Pennsylvania. Like so much of the cottage art of this region, the quilts range from the bold and exuberant to the simple, forthright and unpretentious. The use of color might have been limited by religious dictum—for a Shaker, a combination of more than three colors was considered

A *Star of Bluegrass* quilt covers this mahogany pencil-post bed. A Staffordshire washbowl and pitcher sit on the nightstand. An antique doll rests on the captain's chair at the left of a window outfitted with white louver shutters.

blasphemous. The result is the artful use of drab and strong throughout a pattern that startles the onlooker. Other pious quilt makers made one block, usually in a corner, that didn't quite match the others. This one offending square was stitched into the quilt just in case a ferocious God was affronted by perfection.

All over the nation, during the nineteenth century and well into the twentieth, needles and scissors flashed the winter away, patches stitched into blocks, blocks into quilt tops, and quilt tops to backing. A lot of this went on at social gatherings, the rare opportunities women had to sit down with other women and, with the excuse of honest labor, commune with one another. Quilting was a joy, not a task. No wonder the stitches are so small and so many!

Quilt patterns were named according to geography and local custom. Most of the patterns were copies of what women saw as people passed through their lives or as they themselves passed through the country on the way to one West-lying promised land or another. A few women in the East copied their designs from magazines like *Godey's Lady's Book* and other promoters of European culture. Although these were often beautiful, they were not so truly American in their concepts as patterns called Log Cabin, Barn Raising, Straight Furrow, and Kansas Trouble.

Rural life was reflected in other pattern names too: Wild Goose Chase, School House, Indian Hatchet, Bear's Paw, Melon Patch, Streak of Lightning, Arrowhead, Prickly Path. Some designs have different names in different parts of the country: Robbing Peter to Pay Paul became Lending and Borrowing on the frontier, where people learned they had to cooperate in order to survive. What unhappy woman first named Streak of Lightning the Drunkard's Path? And who was it, so far away from home, who first called her meandering pattern of squares Trip Around the World?

Pretension was not encouraged in rural America, especially along the frontier, where the word *salon* became "saloon" and the quilt pattern called Star of LeMoyne became Lemon Star.

Historical events were also turned into patchwork patterns: there was the popular Burgoyne Surrounded, a single red square boxed in by irregular squares of blues and browns. Maybe it was so popular because most country people had more denim and homespun than cochineal-dyed scarlet cloth. Religion was another favorite theme: many a homesteader slept through the night covered by a Jacob's Ladder or Star of Bethlehem.

Often, in the mid to late nineteenth century, a rural family worked through the winter preparing to pull up stakes and head West the following spring. When they joined wagon trains at Independence, Missouri for the Oregon or the California trail, women from the East exchanged quilt patterns with pioneer women from Illinois or Georgia. Art at the crossroads: like the American basket, the American patchwork quilt benefited in its design by the exchange of ideas that took place during our period of expansion.

From the 1840s to the turn of the century, the American patchwork quilt, like all the other decorative arts, was affected by Victorian fashion. It was easy to gussy up a patchwork quilt: out came the silk, the damask, the embroidery, bits of lace and ribbon, buttons and bows. Although some of these Victorian "high taste" quilts are amusing if not laughable, they are definitely an acquired taste. As an ornamental relic of a culture-conscious time—a bit of showoff from your own ancestors, perhaps—the Victorian quilt is loved and used by many a Down Home decorator. Whether to acquire one is a decision that must be made by consulting one's private memories. If an ornamental Victorian quilt reminds you of Santa and his reindeer, gingerbread men and boughs of holly, then buy it as a bit of your own past made tangible.

The twentieth century's Depression era was a sad one for quilt art. The pieces are faded, the colors drab, and the pieces irregular and small. Seams were no wider than a pencil, and much of the fabric was the cheapest money could buy. Even the stitching is sparse: mostly straight lines crisscrossing to make diamonds, as thread was also dear. Many are done in the crazy-quilt style, which was not put together in blocks so much as simply added to, whenever circumstances changed and a bit of cloth passed into the lowly ragbag. Crazy-quilt pieces were stitched together in something that could only be called geometric chaos, yet some of them are stunning.

Quilts continued to be handmade until World War II. Some of the very recent ones are miracles of optic art, as modern as Andy Warhol. An exceptionally effective optic design is called Baby Blocks; it consists of rows of four-sided blocks laid out on the bias with a combination of dark solid and print that is dizzying in its effect. It is one quilt that deserves to be hung on the wall and appreciated like a painting.

The untold millions of patchwork quilts that were made in this country during the past two centuries have for the most part returned to dust. They were washed in strong brown soap and whipped dry in the wind, used until they became frayed, used again as quilt backing, then relegated to the porch

as casual throw blankets when they became worn again, or perhaps to the field where babies could play on them while mother worked.

The lowly patchwork quilt was not something that was carefully packed away out of the damp for future generations. With the exception of the best quilts—those for the guest or bridal bed, which may have been preserved for sentimental reasons—most of these quilts were purely utilitarian. Some survivors were passed down to affluent descendants who didn't want to throw out an heirloom but were also a little ashamed to have anything so homely and old-fashioned on the bed. Many languished in boxes or were tucked into a tight cedar chest, in the attic, while the downstairs residents slept between satin sheets and machine-made bedding. Then one day yet another descendant found the old forty-niner quilt in the attic, pulled it out, and held it to her heart.

But such discoveries are now most unusual. How many Irish Puzzles, Indian Trails, Ship's Wheels or Harvest Suns were cut up and used as ironing pads or birthing cloths, or for a dog's bed? Enough to keep the price up for the patchwork collector.

Today, fortunately, the craft, along with a lot of other traditional American needlecrafts, is being revived all over the country. The contemporary patchwork artist has the luxury of buying whole cloth, choosing her (or his) colors before choosing a pattern, and using dacron filler, which is much easier to sew through than the cotton or wool used in the traditional quilt. Progress is an American trait, and there are many people who refuse to be purist and see nothing wrong with sleeping under dacron. But the quilt's color scheme will be more successful if the top is made of all-natural fabrics. A patchwork quilt in electric polyester colors or a too-modern print offends many a Down Home eye. Buy a quilt with care; study as many of the antique variety as you can find before you investigate the contemporary market.

The buyer of a patchwork quilt will quickly become fascinated by the work that went into it. The designs are the first to claim attention. Some geometrics look for all the world like a kind of space-age circuit unit. Others create a subtle optical illusion by varying the use of hues or print. Still others use repetition in a stylized, modernistic way. The geometric tulip or basket blocks repeated row upon row rival Warhol's use of repetition. Some designs are quizzical puzzles-within-puzzles called Kaleidoscope or Barn Raising. Step back from them and they start to move, changing form, shape and color as you shift your attention from one element of the design to the next.

When you inspect the quilt closely, another kind of wonder is born. Look at the number of infinitesimal stitches executed in intricate sworls and feathery patterns. Anyone who has stitched several layers of fabric together knows how laboriously those tiny stitches were made. Some designs are filled with triangular pieces that required another kind of skill to keep the bias from stretching. The circle pieces of an appliqué were snipped and turned, tucked and stitched into perfectly smooth circular lines.

The size of a patchwork quilt can be a problem. A really old one will be oversized now because it was made to cover the high beds of earlier times. Victorian quilts may not have been designed to cuddle under so much as to be displayed at the end of a couch or bed. These smaller versions can still be used to drape over a couch or a rocker or on a child's bed, and the larger ones on an outsized bed.

If you are lucky enough to have inherited a family quilt, cherish it. In many ways, the bits of cloth cut from garments your forebears wore have made the quilt more personal than a family portrait. "That's the dress Great-Aunt Silvie wore the day her daddy came home from Appomattox," said a Georgia woman, her voice rich with reminiscence, to a group of strangers coming through her bedroom on a house tour.

Who knew whether she was reciting fact or fiction? Was the bit of lilac print really part of her heritage? No matter. The quilt to her was a treasure, an intimate gift to her from her own past.

*This 1790 four-poster bed, still wearing its original green paint, features an American quilt in blues, pinks and soft beiges. The hooked rug dates from 1850. The night table is a cherry candle stand with a spoke foot.*

89

The quilt on this pine acorn bed is called Drunkard's Path. The blanket chest at the foot of the bed is from the home of Booker T. Washington. Note how patches of antique quilts have been framed and used for wall décor above the headboard.

This guest room in the home of Washington Irving at Sleepy Hollow is painted hunter green with white trim. The white-background American quilt adds a bright sparkle, as do the antique accessories and lightly curtained windows. The dark walls need the strong touch of white.

Antique quilts grace the cannonball beds in this West Virginia farmhouse. Quilts on twin beds need not match, but they should be color-coordinated. The colors in the cotton rug at the foot of the bed facing the fireplace relate to those of the bedcovers and quilts.

Antique quilts are not just for bedcovers. Here a colorful quilt lends country magic to a round dining table.

Weaving has become a new Down Home craft. At Stissing Mountain Craftsmen in upstate New York, weavers create fabrics for clothing and for homespun bedspreads and pillow covers. Today's ragbag art may have come from this loom.

# *Country Wood*

> "It is remarkable what a value is still put upon
> wood even in this age and in this new country,
> a value more permanent and universal than that of
> gold."

*Henry David Thoreau*
Walden

Wood is as natural a part of a country home as geraniums, sunlight, and the aroma of fresh-baked bread. Environmentally, of course, wood is a sound choice for decorative and functional use because it is an organic product that continually renews itself as long as it is harvested with care. Nowhere do environmentally appropriate products look better than in a Down Home setting, and decorating around wood is a pleasure, because wood richly enhances color and texture and, like anything else organic, takes to light, whether natural or incandescent.

As Thoreau observed more than a hundred years ago, wood has always been an American passion. Its grains, its hues and other varying properties are what make it so versatile and so interesting. California redwood, Southern cedar, New England maple, Minnesota log, Oregon fir: indigenous American wood is as diverse as it is abundant. What varieties did not grow

*There's nothing to compare with the country charm of a barn-red house with white-painted flower boxes at the windows. And, to complete the picture, a homemade bird house in the maple tree outside the kitchen window, and a country cat —whose name just might be "Snowy" —not far from the kitchen door.*

in North America could be shipped from the West Indies and South America; mahogany from the Caribbean was a favorite veneer in fancier times. This continent was a woodworker's dream, and there is scarcely a kind of wood or use for it that doesn't fit into a Down Home decorating scheme.

American wood is even patriotic: Old Hickory, the Lincoln Log, George Washington's cherry tree. But the tree that really built this nation was pine. Authentic Early American pine, which has a rosy glow, is now extremely rare and costly. Collectors must always be wary that the pine piece commanding such a high price isn't actually an Empire piece that has been dunked in a lake until its veneer has come off. In addition to its rarity, Early American pine is valued for the width of its boards, sometimes as much as three feet across. Pine pieces from the age before the industrial revolution are especially loved for their handmade quality, that lack of precise uniformity, the hand-carved features, the honest, straightforward beauty of their overall design.

But many other woods were used in American country furniture. A skillful craftsman would often combine several different kinds of a single piece, selecting them for their individual qualities. A chair seat of green wood will dry like a vise around its legs. Hickory takes to a curve well, and sweet chestnut is good for bottom pieces because it doesn't rot in the damp. A single chair may have been constructed out of many pieces: the seat of locust, the curved back of hickory, and the legs of sweet chestnut. Beech and ironwood were two other kinds of wood that would tolerate bending without splintering.

Woods were also selected for their colors. Butternut mellows with age to a glossy taffy. Red cedar is streaked with luscious pink. Birch, stained dark, looks a bit like mahogany, and for earlier Americans who couldn't afford the latter, the former served well. Cherry has a beautiful close grain, and its streaks of sapwood are a delicate pink. It is so hard that it resonates when the end grain is tapped, and because of this hardness it can be rubbed to a surface as smooth as glass. Many a country wife polished her cherry furniture with butter and rubbed until she could see her face reflected in the piece she was buffing.

Furniture of sweet chestnut is easy to date, because in the nineteenth century the tree was nearly wiped out by a blight. The color ranges from warm honey to amber, and since the wood was rot-resistant and needed no finish, it was often used for drawers and the sides of furniture. Hickory and white oak are Atlas trees: the hardest and strongest, yet so resilient they can take a steam bath and be bent into shape without splintering. Even when put on a lathe and reduced to a slender spindle, the wood remains strong, so it was often used for legs (or limbs, as they were called in that euphemistic Victorian Age).

Locust is another tough wood; experts say it will last two years longer than stone. Like stone, it also won't take a nail, and was often used as a chair seat or in other places where glue rather than nails was called for.

Imported since the 1600s, mahogany was used in the sophisticated parlors of Back Bay and the Gold Coast, as well as the Henry Jamesian drawing rooms of Manhattan. It was a popular status symbol with the country gentry as well. The mahogany of the West Indies was as much as ten feet in diameter and so dense it could be carved like marble. Because of its enormous girth and its richly variable grain, mahogany was—and is—a popular veneer. Although the South, with its great fondness for furniture of the Empire period, championed mahogany in both town and country, mahogany really says city, not country, to most people. If country to you is Tara, then use mahogany and love it. Just remember that it could overpower a simple piece of Shaker pine.

Maple is as New England as its syrup. It is also shock-resistant and not easily bruised, and as stiff and hard as a Vermont winter. No wonder it was so popular all around the country for so many years. Not long ago, the more flamboyant grains of maple—the birdseye, tiger and curly grains so prevalent today—were out of favor with country dwellers, and acres of beautiful maple wood lie under many layers of paint in country furniture stores all over America.

Oak was an English wood, as English as Henry VIII. Because it splits beautifully along the grain, it was popular for use as paneling, dados and flooring. White oak was a great favorite for tabletops, and was used also for country floors—some of which are every bit as beautiful as the finer pieces of furniture.

But as we said, pine is the wood that built America. The tree, up to 120 feet tall and as much as 5 feet in diameter, yields straight, even grain and colors that range from creamy white to delicate pink as well as the popular rich brown. Pine is also light in weight when well seasoned, and so pine furniture was often built thick and solid. Like cherry, maple, and oak, pine lasted; and country furniture, walls and floors made of these woods are still plentiful.

The wood that was hand-hewn, hand-dovetailed, planed, turned, and carved by a maker's skill has become something to treasure and is unfortunately out of the price range of most Americans. But the look is readily available in less valuable pieces. Even the bogus Early American pine that took a bath in the nearest river to shed itself of its Empire veneer can be enjoyed for its simplified style and sound construction. Even if it's not the real thing and doesn't claim to be. But be careful that you don't pay for something you're not getting.

Old wood may be much dented and warped, its hues darkened with age. Cherish the dents. Modern distressing techniques may try to duplicate old bruises, but they never quite succeed. The country decorator who uses lots of really old wood, whether it's on the floor, the wall or the ceiling or in the furnishings, will never go wrong.

One great advantage in decorating with wood is its affinity for colors. Sunshine colors are wonderful with rich, dark old woods. So are pastel prints. Once you become a lover, it becomes hard to resist wood, especially the authentically old pieces. But with the price of new furniture—which lacks the soul and sheen of the old—as high as it is, why not buy the old piece? Its patina cannot be duplicated.

If you're going to consider using wood in your country home, read on. The next three chapters will tell you everything you need to know about wood floors and furniture and how to care for them.

*Early American pine is valued for its wide—sometimes 3 feet—boards. The original wood steps still take you upstairs in this historic house on Mackinac Island. Simplicity and under-decoration of space allow the beauty of the American interior to show through.*

A collection of American pewter is displayed in this pine cupboard. Pine pieces from the age before the industrial revolution are prized for their handmade quality.

99

*Old wood may be dented and warped, its hues darkened over the years. Cherish the dents! This corner hutch proudly shows its age. Modern distressing techniques applied to newly built furnishings may try to duplicate old bruises, but they never quite succeed.*

*Right: When America thinks kitchen, America thinks Julia Child. Here, in its simple color scheme of blue-greens and yellow, is Julia's country kitchen with its copper pots, its molds and mixing bowls, and of course its bottle of wine. Who wouldn't want to dine in Julia's kitchen?*

The simplicity of this log cabin country kitchen-dining room —
with its cotton rugs and calico prints and the important pickle
barrel —appeals to the lovers of the out-of-doors.

The tree that built America is
the pine. This pine-paneled
kitchen is filled with things
that say country. A copper
pitcher and pans, brass scales
and scoops and wine
strainers, and a copper apple
butter kettle hang from the
mantel below a pine ogee
clock and toleware and tin
molds. A Shaker-style chair
sits beside the fireplace.

*Fresh herbs from the garden spice up our home-grown vegetables. We grow parsley, spearmint, chives, sage and thyme. We use the summer herbs in homemade winter vinegars.*

Wood is as natural to the country home as geraniums, sunlight, or boys with fishing poles. Decorating around it is a joy, because wood enhances color and texture. And because it is organic, it takes to light, whether natural or artificial, as is demonstrated by the beautiful wood structure of the interior of this barn.

105

# Country Floors

The American dream of a better life can be viewed on the floors of its homes, from the swirled sand over tamped earth of Colonial times to the scrolled white wall-to-wall velvet pile of late-twentieth-century America. Like city folks, country dwellers aspired to the pursuit of happiness. Even when all they could afford was tamped earth, Americans applied their inventiveness to making improvements on the meager materials they had to work with.

One of the first improvements was a poured floor—a mixture of soil, lime, clay, and perhaps some smithy's anvil dust—bound together with a liquid such as oxblood or stale milk. This mixture was poured over earth, and behold! a solid floor that could even be polished to just a hint of a gloss when rubbed with a piece of wool. Sand was swept daily over these dirt floors and sworled into interesting patterns. An oxblood floor was rich brown when first poured, then later turned gray. In the South, floors of terrazzo, cool and

*When the Norman Rockwells selected floor coverings for their Stockbridge, Massachusetts, home, they permitted the borders of their beautiful wood floors to show.*
*They chose a pattern of small flowers for the floor of the entry hall between the sitting room/library and the parlor.*

insect-free, were a favorite. These floors were made of a similar mixture, although plaster-of-paris was occasionally added. Shells were sometimes thrown in for a fancy touch. Some of these old earthen floors still exist today, as cool and insect-free as ever.

But most country folk wanted wood underfoot as soon as they could afford it. They may have laid brick or stone in the kitchen or keeping room, but, for the rest of the house, wood was what everyone wanted. When the rotting floorboards in an old house are removed today, one sometimes finds piles of sand beneath, remnants of daily sweeping and sworling. The wood itself often has an intriguing corrugated surface. For many years the wood was probably scoured with sand, water and a stiff brush until the soft parts gave way, leaving only the hard grain. These floors have great character and often retain the pale color of raw wood. Although they may be worn beyond further use as flooring, they should be salvaged for paneling, or for some other less demanding purpose.

The country look in floors is wide, random widths of floorboard throughout the house. Today those early floors are cherished, but if you aren't fortunate enough to have the real thing underfoot, there are prefabricated wood floors that use the random-width style; some even have nonfunctional pegs to simulate the original nail-free country floor.

Unfortunately, we live in an age when almost nothing made with wood compares with products made in the past. The natural effects of aging simply cannot be duplicated. And so the country decorator should keep a vigilant eye out for available old wood. A barn coming down is to the wood lover every bit as joyous an occurrence as when it was raised. All that beautifully weathered wood is a bonanza. Pay close attention to local papers and local gossip and be on the spot when any old building is about to be demolished.

Three hues of wood work especially well as floors in the country. One is the soft honey glow of pine with a touch of henna. Another is a deeply stained floor that gives a room a kind of gravity and looks wonderful with hand-crafted rugs. A third is a bleached floor that has a gray, weathered look. If your house is truly rustic, you might want to keep it that way by applying a white stain to the floor, followed by several coats of polyurethane to keep it clean and shining. This floor is especially good if you want more light in your rooms. Many a country house was built without any windows on the north side so that it would be warmer in the winter. A light-colored floor is one way to intensify the available light.

One favorite ancestral floor treatment for wood was paint. Plain, undecorated floors were often painted in earth colors of terra cotta, clay, brown, ochre, green, gray or blue. These colors still work well today. Extensive use of white is best avoided in the country because it is too sharp for the overall mood. Be sure that the paint color you choose duplicates one of those pre-Chemical Age hues that were clear and deep from natural dyes, not the kind that come in a can of acrylic. Keep nature in mind when you choose a floor color.

Many of our ancestors weren't satisfied with just painting the floor a solid color. Some did free-hand painting of landscapes, flowers, or whatever struck their fancy, often trying to duplicate the pattern of a popular rug. For many a poor country family, a rug painted on the floor took the place of a store-bought one. Some floors were spattered in two colors, marbelized, or painted to look like expensive parquet. (Duplicating expensive styles is an old American tradition.) For some floor painters, the cracks between the boards became the stripes in a geometric design. Painted stair runners could also be

*If you're lucky enough to have a stone floor like this one in your keeping room or kitchen, count your blessings, because craftsmen capable of doing the stone work are hard to find.*

attractive, and were sometimes bordered in a trellis and vine pattern of green over blue. Another popular floor was rust red with a yellow ochre stenciled border of grain sheaves bound with leaves. If you think you'd like a painted floor, consider a stenciling kit. In olden days, the stencil was used on the wall as well as the floor by people who could not afford wallpaper.

Painted floors were popular throughout the nineteenth century, but when machine-made carpets came on the market in mass quantities and the average family could finally afford one of these coveted luxuries, wood went back to being wood. The descendants of carpet painters, having had the Brussels carpets, the aubussons, the flokati, the $25-a-yard-wall-to-wall, and the Persian prayer rugs, are taking another look at painted floors and finding them pleasing in a folksy sort of way.

Wide wood floors as naked as can be: that's a sensible and attractive choice for a dining room. Using a rug under a dining room table is like feeding the baby without a bib: it's just asking for trouble. Everybody spills food now and then, and does a dining room floor today really need to be "warmed"? The idea is not silly, just a little outdated in this age of central heating. Using a rug under the dining room table poses another problem: it looks fine when no one is sitting at the table, but as soon as a chair is pulled out, the back legs extend beyond the rug, and your guests find themselves eating their dinners at a slight tilt. Country life is supposed to be scaled down, simple, and easy on the upkeep. Do yourself a favor by putting the dining room table on a gleaming, highly polished wood floor (of random-width boards, preferably).

A word about wall-to-wall in the country. Everyone enjoys the feel of a soft, warm rug underfoot, most particularly beside the bathtub and the bed. But is it really necessary to cover all those beautiful hardwood floors? Let them show! Why not spend the money for wall-to-wall (and these days that may be the single most expensive item in your decorating budget) on some beautiful hooked, braided, rag or woven rugs, either antique or recently hand-crafted? If you want wall-to-wall anyway, consider a pleasing duplication of nature's own ground cover, and remember that the country is not the place for sculptured pile, velvet or other ostentatious materials.

In the kitchen, a favored choice is stone, brick, or clay tile. It is in the kitchen that our sense memories are most intense, and we are reminded that the floor of poured earth, stone or brick is the oldest one of all. Despite its flintiness, it has a rich, warm look that can never quite be duplicated with manmade materials.

*A rope swing for the children is a must for the Down Home porch. Adults will occupy the more sedate natural-wicker chairs sitting on the gray-painted wood floor.*

*Ah, the open fire! Here, a pair of milking stools are pulled up to the hearth. Stone floors in the kitchen area were practical for the early American homemaker.*

For the kitchen, the most popular floors are of brick or stone or clay tile. The butter churn on this brick floor reminds us of one of the country woman's daily chores. A place is set for lunch amid herb jars and an iron pot.

The gray, weathered look of a bleached floor—the perfect spot for an old barrel—is wonderful in the country. If your house is truly rustic, you might want to apply a white stain to your floor and then seal it with several coats of polyurethane to keep it clean and shining.

*For that bit of warmth underfoot that everyone loves, a
mid-nineteenth-century hooked rug lies on the floor of this
bedroom. An American chintz quilt covers the green-painted
pencil-post bed. The primitive painting of a young girl over
the box-stretcher tavern table is an Erastus Salisbury Field.*

*Floors that retain the pale color of raw wood have great
character. Wide boards of random widths should be used
wherever possible in the Down Home house.*

# Country Floor Coverings

Some time ago, a carpet company came up with the slogan "A title on the door means a [carpet] on the floor." The carpet became a status symbol in the Age of Affluence, and the ultimate status was wall-to-wall. The ultimate color for it was white, to indicate that money was no object and that nothing grubby went on here. This kind of symbolism is totally inappropriate in the country. Anything that smacks of showing off is jarring.

One couple I know bought a New England farmhouse that had beautiful oak floors throughout in a herringbone pattern. They were scratched up and dark but essentially in good shape. Instead of refinishing the wood and giving it a high gloss, the couple covered their entire house, upstairs and down, with very expensive royal red sculptured velvet. Such opera-house opulence on the floors of that staid, sensible old dwelling, with its low ceilings, dormered windows, heavy beams and simple architecture, was nothing less than a disaster.

*For the country house with an American flavor, an Oriental rug could be perfect—with a pine table, Windsor chairs, and an array of lush Boston ferns at the windows.*

The best approach to choosing a country floor covering is to think wood, and then think small rugs. Spend that hefty wall-to-wall sum on those small hand-crafted rugs that look so good on a highly polished wood floor. In keeping with the unifying effect of all-one-color walls, a hardwood floor—exposed upstairs, downstairs and all throughout the house—will pull the rooms together. Smaller rugs will also pull together intimate conversation areas.

The Down Home rug is one that has an interesting texture, clear natural colors, and few pretensions. Preferably, the country rug will be hand-crafted. If it is machine made, it should have an overall look of honest, cheerful simplicity. Natural textures are always best—wool, cotton, flokati, and matting. Nature's own textures can't go wrong on a country floor. The most successful country rug is (or looks like) the one once made at home. Some of the best have become folk art and should be hung on a wall to be admired like a tapestry. The hand-crafted rug was traditionally braided, hooked, woven, or crocheted. In a wide variety of styles—from the woven Navaho rug made of wool, dyed natural colors, to the New Englander's hooked rug of wool or cotton—the hand-crafted rug is available all around the country.

The colors of these rugs are a nice complement to Down Home's general color scheme. The helter-skelter hues of braided and rag rugs, the vivid colors against the dark backgrounds of hooked rugs, the simple but elegant color combinations in a woven Indian rug—what could look better, framed by an expanse of polished honey-colored wood?

The rag rug was a highly popular way of "warming the floor" in the days before cloth was cheap. As with the scraps saved for the patchwork quilt, the ragbag was the source of materials for the rag rug. Pieces too small even for a patchwork quilt were cut into narrow strips, sewn together, then woven on a hand loom, crocheted, knitted or braided. All through the long winter, when the pace of outdoor work on the farm slowed, an entire family might work on rug making. The process was laborious, and a rug normally didn't last long under the heavy-duty wear it got in a country house, but even so, some of these carpets have survived and are today exhibited as works of art, much as the best quilts are.

The Quakers used the selvedge edges of yardgoods for a particularly durable, ravel-free rug. The patterns were often executed in subdued stripes, sometimes fancied up with the embroidery of stencil-like designs or geometrics between stripes. The rug in the parlor, or "best room," might be one of these embroidered affairs, although the time consumed by making such a rug took it out of the realm of possibility for many country wives busy with house, garden, barn, dairy and children.

The rag carpet, in addition to being a pleasure to look at, is durable. For one thing, it is reversible. It's also often washable, and with a pad underneath to keep the rug from slipping, it can be used and appreciated nearly anywhere in the house, from an entryway to an attic guestroom.

The braid is one of the most ancient methods of employing several parts to make a strong whole. The raw ends are neatly tucked under as the strips are folded into the braid, and then the braids are blindstitched or laced together into rounds or ovals. For many years now, braided rugs have been made by machine, but they have never quite matched the quality of the no-stitch-showing hand-crafted ones.

The knitted or crocheted rug was also a product of the ragbag. Instead of braiding or weaving the strips together, the rug maker used a crochet or knitting hook. Lightweight material such as denim or calico would be used in these rugs, since such fabrics were easier to take up on a hook. Many of the patterns, like those of braided or woven rag rugs, were hit-and-miss, although the more affluent rug maker sometimes had enough fabric in different colors to plan an overall design. Some of these hooked rag rugs were embroidered in the center, crocheted in the middle, or knitted in narrow strips which were fastened like spokes to a wheel and given a border. These small, cheerful rugs are perfect all through a country house, where they truly warm the floor with their unpretentious and honest glow. Rags they may have been, but someone thrifty with an eye toward beauty made them into a thing of value.

For the hooked rug, small strips of fabric were brought through an open-weave backing such as burlap with a special hook. If the creator had talent and imagination, the design might be original. The family dog, the homestead, the home state territory, or a slogan like "54-40 or Fight" might be worked into the rug. If the rug maker needed an inspiration, stenciled burlap backing was available which delineated a host of popular Oriental patterns as well as lions, patriotic symbols, or the fruit-and-flower motifs so dear to the Victorian heart. For many a country dweller with high hopes for the future but an empty pocket, the hooked rug was as close as the family ever came to walking on pile. Some rugs had a fluffy nap made by unraveling the strips of cotton. Other thrifty extravaganzas were room size and took years to complete.

Another popular carpet of the nineteenth-century home was the ravel-knit rug. It looked remarkably like the contemporary Danish rya rug. These rather flamboyant pieces (strangely enough, many of them are thought to be Shaker) were made of knitted scraps that had been unraveled until they produced a deep shag pile.

Other hand-crafted American rugs that work well in a country home are the woven wool rugs of the Navaho and Hopi Indians. One popular kind was called the jerga, a flat-woven rug made to be thrown over tamped earth. This jerga originated in Spain and was brought to the New World by the white conquerors. Made of wool from the Indians' own herds, these rugs were woven in stripes, checks, twill or herringbone patterns in the wonderful natural sheep colors of cream to brown to black, plus the rich red made from the cochineal and indigo dye imported from Mexico. To provide additional padding over the tamped earth, the jerga was often installed wall-to-wall over freshly sheared wool. Good facsimiles of the jerga are available in a variety of sizes.

The Navaho and Hopi Indians weave their legends into their rugs, and each pattern has a symbolic meaning as old as their cultures. A rug may tell the story of Spider Man and the loom he built for Spider Woman, or it may simply be called Two Gray Hills. Its diamonds, suns, mountains or streaks of lightning may be designed so that no matter how the rug is folded, the design is pleasing, which makes the rug perfect for folding at the end of a bed.

The Navahos were sheepherders, and the abundance of wool and the great demand for their product have turned rug making into an art as well as an industry. Their rugs are often still made from scratch by hand—from shearing to carding, spinning, dyeing and weaving. People who own these rugs often consider them much too beautiful and valuable to be used on the floor. Fortunately, they look splendid on either a wall or a bed.

There is yet another kind of floor covering that has plenty of historical precedence in a Down Home setting, and that is matting.

Woodland Indians, using simple looms, interwove strips of cedar bark, often in patterns of light and dark. Mats were also made of plaited rush, woven grasses or even cornhusks. When the first Europeans came to the New World, they too used matting: the earliest record of this kind of floor covering in the New World dates from the 1620s. Matting was popular in the early days of America because it was made with materials that were much cheaper and more plentiful than cloth. Straw, cattails, sedge, jute and sisal, as well as grasses and cornhusks, were in abundance. A cornhusk mat at the door not only provides interest, but does a good job of removing dirt from shoes.

*Original designs were often worked into hooked rugs by talented Down Home creators. Here a hearthside rug made by an imaginative country lady warms the stone floor beside a handmade child's chair. The rug is multicolored and features reds, golds, yellows and greens on a beige ground.*

Since dirt was also plentiful in those days, matting was a sensible floor covering: rugs could periodically be taken up and cleaned while the dirt and dust beneath them were swept out. Since soap turned the mats yellow, they were cleaned with cornmeal and water. Some were even varnished. George Washington ordered many yards of matting for Mount Vernon. Matting was also used as a base for smaller rugs, and in many households cloth area rugs were taken up in the spring and put down again in the winter to save wear and tear on the rugs.

Matting is again enormously popular. It succeeds in a Down Home environment because of its natural colors and textures, and it still enhances the look of an area rug thrown over it.

Yet another kind of floor covering has its origins deep in American history, although its latest derivative, vinyl, certainly doesn't remind most people of authentic country style. Nevertheless, the ancestor of cushion vinyl and peel-and-stick tile was a canvas floor covering that dates back to the early eighteenth century, perhaps even before. The canvas was coated to make it moisture proof and was used to protect the wood underneath. It was especially popular in hallways and on stairs. Sometimes it was also used over expensive carpets and under dining room tables.

Oilcloth was an improvement over the old painted canvas, and was also in use as early as Colonial times. Linen or cotton fabric was treated with a waterproofing mixture of oil, glue, and a resin, and the cloth was then painted to look like wood floors or rugs. Often oilcloth was stenciled with borders, given an imitation marble look or painted free-hand.

There are still people in certain parts of the Bronx and Brooklyn who call linoleum "earlcloth." By the twentieth century, American homes in both city and country were being covered wall to wall, room to room, with linoleum. If the linoleum didn't extend wall to wall, people often painted the wood around it, as if the wood had somehow become an embarrassment. Some linoleum managed to look ruglike, but most of it was ugly stuff. Many a country decorator has had to remove untold layers of linoleum before hitting paydirt—floorboards that hadn't seen the light of day for generations.

Those who are partial to the work-saving features of "earlcloth," available today in a staggering variety of colors and designs, use it in a country home with the knowledge that there is plenty of historical precedent. But with the advent of supertough varnishes, exposing the beautiful hardwood floors found in so many older country houses seems like a more reasonable alternative. A well-varnished wood floor is just as easy to keep clean as one of cushion vinyl. Still, if vinyl awakens your sense memories to some warm feeling of another floor from another time, by all means choose it. The choices include many styles that imitate (some successfully, others not) nature's own colors and textures.

What could be more pleasing than a country house with a gleaming hardwood floor upstairs and down, covered here and there with vivid, colorful rugs small enough to take a beating—literally—on the clothesline with an antique wire beater that hangs on the wall as an *objet d'art*? Beating probably gets out more dirt than any vacuum cleaner ever could. Smaller rugs, particularly those with borders, lend themselves well to the overall plan of creating intimate areas throughout a house—to use for conversation, work, reading or unwinding. And your decision to use small rugs guarantees you the fun of browsing around flea markets and going to auctions in search of irresistible bargains. Whether hooked, crocheted, braided, or woven, these rugs have enough character to go around. They also glorify the country tradition of "Waste not, want not" in a way that sculptured velvet pile never could.

*The hand-crafted rug in front of this country fireplace features a flower motif of reds and white on a black background. The ladder-back chair with sausage turnings dates from 1760. The handmade lantern beside the chair is painted tin. The andirons are original Hessian soldiers.*

The country kitchen of famed collector Ruth Gordon Ellis is furnished with a shoe-foot hutch table dated 1750; its Windsor chairs, one of which is painted, date to 1760. The furnishings rest on a Heriz rug in the serape pattern.

Nature's own textures can't go wrong on a country floor. This rug of natural matting in a plaid design can be used in any room of the Down Home dwelling, from living room to kitchen and on to the bedroom.

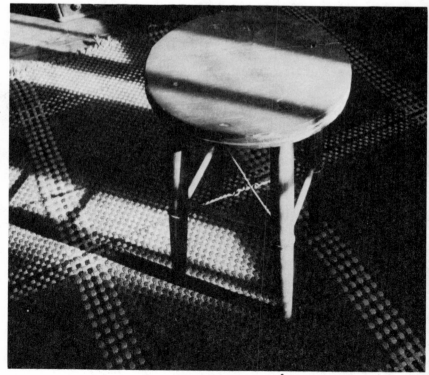

*Americans enjoy hand-crafted braided, hooked, woven or crocheted rugs. Here a vividly colored braided rug is used in a country dining room on a honey-colored polished wood floor. A pine dining table with benches and Windsor chairs completes the setting.*

# Country Furniture

"Of simple life and country ways . . ."
*John Greenleaf Whittier*
Snowbound

The Shaker philosophy of furniture making was to work as if you had a thousand years to live and yet as if you were going to die tomorrow. The result, for most people, is the best of country furniture—pure and simple and durable. Not that all country furniture adheres to the Shaker philosophy of unadorned simplicity. Some pieces are impossibly ornate, others are simply too big for a scaled-down country room, and still others are poorly crafted. Styles and quality vary widely, but one thing nearly all country furniture *is* is wood.

"In oak and walnut
Those old New England carpenters
 hoisted and wrought.
Sunup till sundown they hoisted. . . ."

*Carl Sandburg*
The People, Yes

*An arrangement of cut garden flowers brightens this English oak side table with its American student lamp. The flooring is a herringbone pattern of brick.*

If there was one resource aplenty in the Land of Plenty, it was wood, and much of the furniture our forebears made, from the earliest Colonial times to the Victorian Age, is now cherished for its sturdy craftsmanship, attention to fine detail, quality hardware, pleasing style, and patina—the incomparable look of a fine old piece of wood. Country furniture is loved for every nick and worn spot, so loved in fact that contemporary pieces are sometimes turned out artificially distressed: attacked with mallets and lengths of chain to make them look like old pieces. They never do, and if you believe in karma you wouldn't want to live with a piece of furniture that had been beaten!

Many home decorators are afraid of living with antique furniture. What is an antique, anyway? Traditionally, it's something at least a hundred years old, although that cutoff continually shifts, depending on the category of the antique. Too many people think of an antique chair, for instance, as something spindly that would crash to the floor if you didn't lower yourself into it very gently. Nothing could be further from the truth if the antique is a sturdy Down Home piece of furniture, for the typical American country piece is hardly ever the la-di-da type that was built strictly for show.

Country furniture was made to last, to pass on to future generations of robust, hard-working farm people. Of course it was also bought or made for its beauty, but country people also needed tables, for example, that were big enough and wide enough to support a hearty meal for eight or ten. Country chairs were built to take a little overflow. Country chests were wide and roomy because many were substitute closets. Country furniture was built to be sturdy, and was as comfortable as our comfort-shunning ancestors could tolerate.

This kind of furniture, often encrusted with layers of varnish or paint, awaits the Down Home decorator in out-of-the-way places across the country. It is also available cleaned up and at a higher price in urban antique stores. Wherever you wish to go hunting, choosing the right pieces is a joy. They call to you, awakening pleasant memories that will practically make your decisions for you. Whether it's a spindle bed high off the floor, a round oak table, or a Duncan Phyfe sofa, there are certain kinds of furniture that have the built-in charm of childhood memory. This sense memory factor is not to be taken lightly when looking for country furniture. A home is to be happy in, and certain pieces of furniture are easy to love.

From plain to fancy, simple pine to ornate Victorian, there is a country furniture style to suit anyone's taste. The earliest pieces of Americana are now housed in museums, but furniture styles continued to be copied long after the original "name" maker had gone to his reward, so buying authentic country furniture doesn't mean spending a fortune on signed quality pieces. It means keeping an eye out for a fine "contemporary" reproduction of a Hitchcock chair, or a Queen Anne wingback, or a Shaker bench with pristine lines. A coveted style is imitated, and we are the beneficiaries.

The first American furniture was whatever a colonist had managed to bring from Europe. Settlers were forced then either to pay high import prices or make their own. Furniture that came from the old country was highly prized: Queen Anne, Hepplewhite and Sheraton were styles that even fervent anti-Royalists coveted. But by the late eighteenth century, America had its own superior craftsman—Duncan Phyfe. Then, around 1820, the first quality piece of mass-produced furniture was turned out in a factory in Riverton, Connecticut. It was a chair named for its maker, Lambert Hitchcock.

Hitchcock's factory was the bellwether of the industrial revolution in the new country. The Hitchcock chair was so popular that the factory began shipping parts to furniture makers in all sections of the country. Like all his American competitors, Hitchcock was influenced by British furniture design, but he is still called the father of the American chair, and his method of mass-producing quality meant that many people, not just a privileged few, could afford at least one piece of good furniture.

Such country antiques are still valued, of course, but it is the earliest, pre-machine-age pieces that are valued most. They were made by hand with plane, drawknife, rasp and file, turned by hand on a lathe, carved and planed and burnished. Wood, being organic, requires the human capacity to respond to the unexpected. Wood is not uniform, and so furniture made by hand often isn't either, but it is the individual nonstandardized look of the handmade piece that makes it so cherished.

Whether the antique was handmade or mass-produced, it is sure to have been carefully made. Its mortise-and-tendon joints were executed with skill; its shell-carved drawer front was a work of pride. A table may have been given a slight rise in its dropleaf to compensate for the sag that often occurs when that kind of table is extended. Its country burrs were all well burnished. Furniture was made with much attention to practical detail: back legs, particularly those of highboys and backboards, were made straight so they would stand flush against the wall.

There are some expensive pieces that are called Early American that are actually Victorian or Empire pieces stripped of their geegaws and veneer. As pine was the base wood for many veneered pieces, a suitably old piece

*No Down Home dining area is complete without a hutch. Hutches remained popular throughout the nineteenth century as receptacles of affluence, growing bigger as the country itself grew; and many styles are still available. This corner cupboard has its original hinges and original paint.*

stripped of its trimming may fool the unwary. If you're about to buy a piece of alleged Early American, it's wise to call in an expert. On the other hand, if the price is right, a piece of stripped-down nineteenth-century furniture may look fine in your country house—as long as you're not paying for Early American!

All across the U.S., people are going country. Golden oak is all the rage in Dallas and Seattle, and the Far West look is framed in the windows of antique shops in Greenwich Village. Victorian is gaining in popularity; and Empire, which has always been a favorite in the South, is also being revived, although its massiveness may not be suited to the typically small country room of colder climes.

In the next few pages, different kinds of country furniture will be described room by room, but no matter where it is used, Down Home furniture should be arranged with a thought to a commingling of body heat. In the days before central heating, furniture was best arranged in intimate clusters for warmth and conversation. The same holds true today as energy costs spiral upward. Clustering furniture around fireplaces is easy, but the same inviting look should prevail throughout the house.

Have a party. Extend it to every room. Bid your guests good night and go to bed. Get up (late) and walk through your house. See how your guests have left the furniture. Consider keeping the arrangement permanent, with a little adjustment for traffic areas and a minimum of thought to symmetry. This idea is especially good for country houses with large open spaces that need to be made more intimate. The mingling of body heat is a good thing—winter and summer—and formality in the country is best left to your tuxedoed cat.

## Dining Furniture

Whether you dine in the kitchen, the dining room or a combination living-and-dining area, your table and chairs should meet certain requirements: they should expand to feed a lot of people (unless your country house is a retreat from entertaining, in which case you may buy a smaller table and never have the option to throw a big bash), and everyone should be able to sit comfortably. The most popular dining tables are, of course, sturdy, solid wood, whether golden oak, round as the sun with lion's claws, a gateleg or splay-legged dropleaf table, a tavern table, trestle table or Pennsylvania Dutch table with free-standing legs. Your choice can be as simple as several long pine planks or as elegant as a two-part Empire table with reeded legs and brass feet.

Real wood can't miss. You can serve meals on the bare table or on cloth placemats and the wood will shine through, as it will through a lacy, spidery crocheted tablecloth. Somehow (perhaps it's sense memory again) food tastes better when it's served on a wood tabletop.

It's good to avoid the "suite" look in dining furniture for the country. If there's one place everything *doesn't* have to match, it's Down Home. Not even the dining chairs have to be alike. You can try using a combination of chairs and benches around your groaning board. A deacon's bench—of about the same length as your rectangular table, for instance—can be used against a wall in combination with Hitchcock chairs or ladderbacks with rush seats. Patchwork is effective on cushions in a country dining spot, and a bench could use the kind of comfort a cushion provides. You might want to use patchwork valances and tablecloth to pull the area together.

Benches are as country as church and garden paths. In fact, church pews, made more comfortable with a cushion, can make excellent dining benches. Have the bench sawed off to the length you want and replace its arm at the cut. If a church bench isn't to your taste, there are also captain's benches, wicker benches, and even old-fashioned buggy seats mounted on legs. A simple outdoor bench made of a log nailed to four hand-hewn legs is another possibility. If you want something more refined, consider a Hitchcock-type stenciled settee.

The dining chair is one of those categories of furniture which may offer too many bewildering choices for the novice country furniture buyer. So many styles! You can make your task easier from the beginning by eliminating all those dining chairs that aren't really comfortable. A favorite choice for the comfort-conscious is an armchair, and few will surpass the Windsor chair for comfort. Although the name conjures up royalty, and the style did originate in England, its origins here were more democratic. The Windsor chair was the favorite at the tavern or meeting hall. And no wonder. With its arched back and generous, deep-cut seat, it is one of the most comfortable pieces of wood ever turned into something to sit on. For all its comfort, it was sturdy enough not to collapse when a well-fed burgher tipped himself back on its two graceful back legs. Its strength lay in the combination of woods that went into it, each chosen for its special properties. Easy-to-bend hickory went into the arched back; and maple, because it turns well, was used in the stretchers. The seat was probably pine, a wood soft enough to scoop out a comfortable resting place for a hungry owner, an owner's children, and their children's grandchildren. The combination of woods was so skillfully executed that a two-hundred-year-old Windsor chair is likely still to have all its rungs and spindles intact. So much for the fragility of antiques! Because of its multi-wood derivation, the Windsor was usually painted black and stenciled. It still looks best that way, although the tendency these days is to strip and varnish it.

The captain's chair with arms is another choice that stays comfortable all through after-dinner conversation. Often made of a softer wood than pine, and not so slender in its turnings as the Windsor, the captain's chair is still remarkably popular.

The ladderback chair, which dates from the nineteenth century, is truly American. An early one will show wear, of course, and the rush seat may have been replaced many times. Fortunately, with the revival of interest in all things American, there has also been an increase in the number of craftspeople who can work with cane, rush, and other fibrous seating materials. The Sheraton-style chair is another shapely dining choice, as are arrow back, fiddle back, comb back, and the elaborately carved Victorian side chair. Make your choice by taking into consideration the size of your dining area (you don't want to overwhelm the room with chairs), the comfort and the looks that really please you.

No dining area is complete without a sideboard or hutch—another item of Down Home furniture available in many styles. Every farm family of yore, once it began to prosper, wanted a nice piece of furniture with some open shelving or glass doors which would display a new set of willow or mochaware. Hutches remained popular through the nineteenth century as receptacles of affluence, growing bigger as the country itself grew. Your choice can be anything from the simplest New England pine trestle table to the most ornate Chippendale-style carved cherry corner cupboard with graceful fluted columns and fancy hinges. In between the plain and fancy are mahogany sideboards in Hepplewhite or Sheraton style, folksy cupboards from the kitchen with open shelves on top and enclosed cupboards beneath, or a large Pennsylvania dresser with paneled doors, open shelves and even a spoon rack. Keep your china collectibles in mind when choosing your dining closet. Although the piece doesn't have to match, it should complement your other dining room furniture.

**The Living Room**

The style of the old-fashioned parlor is one best left to dim memory. There was nothing very comfortable about the best room, where our ancestors entertained the minister, the teacher, and other people too important to bring into the kitchen. Comfort was not the main consideration; respectability was. Now that people aren't so anxious about being judged by their furniture, the parlor or (for lack of a better word) the living room (in a country home, living goes on in *every* room) can be anything you want it to be, as long as it meets certain Down Home qualifications of comfort, style and a sense of history.

You may want to indulge yourself in one truly sensational piece—a mid-nineteenth-century medallion-back Victorian sofa, for instance, or an Empire cornucopia couch. Or you may want to stick with the solid comfort of a traditional pillow-backed sofa and combine it with some period pieces. Comfortable upholstered chairs include a Queen Anne-style wingback, a heart-back Hepplewhite-style armchair, or a late-Victorian gentleman's chair.

Freely consult your sense memory when selecting furniture for this room. The grand curves of a Victorian sofa awaken pleasant memories for many people for whom its old-fashioned opulence represents Christmas in the country, Currier and Ives, and a gentler time when people had morning rooms and drawing rooms, wrote letters instead of calling by telephone, and spent hours in their rose gardens. Fortunately, these couches are easy to plan a room around, and they mix well with pieces from other eras, just as they did in our grandparents' parlor.

A living room needs some small tables on which to set drinks, ashtrays, coffee cups and lamps. Fortunately, these antiques are easy to find because every home before Edison had many small candle stands. Larger but still narrow tavern or trestle tables work well behind a couch, and sawed-off cobbler's benches are still popular as coffee tables. You may be able to satisfy your heart's desire with something graceful and marble-topped.

If there is a fireplace, you may want to group your favorite pieces around it. Sofas usually work best when they're not so all alone against one wall. Smaller sofas or love seats are often preferred because a sofa is rarely used by more than two people anyway. A pair of small country sofas can face each other across a fire, perhaps with a coffee table between them. End tables generally work best when they are of the same height even if they don't match and are set at the sides of the couches nearest the fireplace.

Nor do the lamps have to match, although they too should be generally about the same height. Turn to "Country Lights" for inspiration on how to light your living room.

A rocker is a natural by the fireplace, and it is a good pull-up chair in a

Blue and white has been a favorite color scheme of the country homemaker for generations. Here, the ever popular blue and white gingham check is used on a pillow lightly tossed against the brick-colored seat cushion of the high-back settee. Wood beams add further to the authentic country look of the room, as does the blue and white Canton and Delft display in the Welsh cupboard.

135

country living room. Boston and Salem immediately come to mind. Like the Windsor chair, these rockers were designed with the human body in mind: wide enough for comfort, yet with a feeling of solidity to match their fine and graceful lines. It's said that the Boston rocker, with its familiar carved seat and back, turned legs and rolled armrests, is the most popular chair ever invented. It's also one of the most satisfying to sit and rock in—at any age. But a scrolled Victorian mahogany may be more your style, or a carved Pennsylvania rocker with a plaited rush back. When new babies were frequent arrivals, every farmhouse had a sturdy rocker, and many of them are still around in a wide range of prices.

Once you have selected the furniture pieces for your Down Home living room, you can turn to "Country Collectibles" for some ideas for accessories as well as to other chapters in this book that cover walls, lighting fixtures, fireplaces, floors and floor covering. The look you are aiming for is the comfort and coziness of the old-fashioned keeping room. The great advantage of today's living room, of course, is that it eliminates the congestion of one-room living, and is away from cooking grease and smells. The formal parlor look will not do these days, but the graciousness of the parlor as a place to bring honored guests is certainly appropriate.

There may be a room in your country home close to the living room or kitchen that you can turn into a library.

"The Almanac we studied o'er,
Read and reread our little store,
Of books and pamphlets, scarce a score;
One harmless novel, mostly hid
from younger ages, a book forbid,
And poetry, (or good or bad,
a single book was all we had)."

One has to prepare for being snowbound in the country, and you will certainly want to avoid the meager fare John Greenleaf Whittier describes above. A country library is a joy to decorate because country desks and bookcases are so pleasing in their variety and style. After all, the desk was an important piece of furniture in a country home because there was much record keeping connected with rural life: the date when the incubator was set, how much hay was put up, how much seed was ordered. In the days

*For the country house with the English flavour, an Oriental rug could be perfect, along with some yew wood chairs.*

Overleaf: *My favorite room in our 1795 farmhouse is the living room. In restoring the house, we removed all the white-painted wallboard from the ceiling and found the beams and boards we so enjoy. We left them just as they were.*

For interesting wall décor, consider an English spoon rack on which you can display your prized pewter objects. The hanging dried peppers bring a touch of nature into this room.

before the telephone, there were also a lot of letters to write. A great favorite is the rolltop desk, that marvelous filing system of little cubbyholes and drawers. The rolltop desk is popular not only for its beauty and convenience but for the slatted top that conceals the mess within! A rolltop sells at whatever the market will bear, and because of its great popularity you must be prepared to pay a premium price.

Fortunately, there are many tempting alternatives. Someone who can't work at a cramped little desk may want to consider an expansive Empire piece or a nineteenth-century pine schoolmaster's desk. If space is a problem, look at hingetop desks or a "desk box" that can be set anywhere and used as a writing surface by opening its hinge. A lover of Victoriana might be drawn to the idea of addressing Christmas cards on a gently curving mahogany-veneered bombé desk with ornate hardware.

A desk needs a chair, and again there is a high premium on comfort. Many armchairs will fit the bill, from a tidy little Sheraton side chair with arms to an expansive oak slatback on a swivel base. You will also be drawn to the many glassed-in bookcases so popular with our ancestors, some leaded or nicely beveled. Or you may want to install a wall of built-in old pine shelving.

After all, you need a home for that well-chosen collection of country books. You don't want to be caught in a snowstorm or face a rainy weekend with nothing but a *Nancy Drew* and last week's paper. The country bookcase is for those uplifting books you never quite get around to reading in the city. It's most certainly for poetry, and for bird and wildflower identification books. And it should include books that are meant to be read aloud: selections from Dickens, Twain, Conan Doyle, or Emily Bronte. Finally, you need a few children's books, a medical guide, a home emergency guide, a farmer's almanac, and some gardening books.

If you can manage it, choose for the library a room that has a fireplace. Anyone who loves a good book and a glass of Amaretto before going to bed would enjoy them most in the country before a fire. Why not provide for such yearnings? The country library can be your little indulgence; our ancestors couldn't afford the space or time to devote to reading that we can. Once you review your dimensions and needs, you will find that your country library decorates itself, and another keeping room may be in the making.

**The Bedroom**

For generations, all but the wealthy slept wherever they could best take advantage of the fire's dying warmth. Peasants slept above the store, an ac-

An American Hepplewhite pine hunt board graces the foyer of this West Virginia country home. The pictures of Martha and George Washington date to 1880; the chair is an original Shaker piece. The antique basket on the floor below the hunt board holds the family's mittens, scarfs and winter caps. Down Home folk make their houses work for their needs —charmingly.

commodating arrangement, but others were more likely to sleep in the room they lived in, much as many people do today who live in studio apartments.

As country people prospered, their houses expanded along with their fortunes. By the time the pious and secretive Victorian Age was reached, a house without a bedroom was unthinkable. But before central heating became widespread, the bedroom remained a place to go to sleep—and through the long, cold part of the year, one jumped into bed under four or five quilts.

Country beds were high, to keep the occupant as far as possible from the drafty floor. They were often enclosed by curtains to keep in body heat, and those curtains may have been embroidered by the mistress of the house. The room might also have contained a big piece of furniture that served as a closet, perhaps even roomy enough to walk into. Bedrooms came before closets: for much of our history, ordinary people couldn't afford to build these little rooms into their houses.

But the memory of a country bedroom in the springtime is something else again—the memory, perhaps, of a lazy afternoon in August when, even though you were down with the measles, you were content just to watch the breeze fluff the lace curtains. The modern country bedroom can be a sitting room, a private salon, a workroom, or just a soft, comfortable room to fall asleep in. The Down Home bedroom is nightcaps and bedside candles, rain on the roof, down and patchwork, sheets dried on the grass in the sun, hoot owls, nightingales, and the cock crowing in the morning. Executing the look is easy once you get the picture: you want a nice high bed piled even higher with patchwork quilts, a roomy painted kas (a Dutch storage chest) in the corner, a shuttered window, and, of course, those lace curtains.

Country beds are laden with importance. After all, people were born in them, died in them, and passed them on to future generations. Boasting that important people slept in one's bed is part of the American culture. "George Washington slept here" is so common a phrase that the father of our country must have done little else than sleep his life away in charming country bedrooms.

Your choices for beds are many and tempting: gleaming brass or painted iron, canopied or four-poster; Pennsylvania Dutch carved with stylized tulips; Jenny Lind, rope, settle, trundle or spool. Country bed frames were made to last, and they belong in one of those categories of furniture in which the old is nearly always preferable to the new. Country beds are often found in solid maple, oak or pine. The high, lavish, and richly carved Empire or

Victorian bedsteads resembling throne backs don't really suit a small room; display them only in a room that befits their grandeur.

As for bedding, that's an easy decision in the country: snow white, all cotton or linen; laces and ruffles; down pillows; patchwork; appliqué; candlewick or maybe old-fashioned chenille.

Since a full cradle was essential to the continuance of a farm family's prosperity, there used to be one in every home. Cradles today can be plain and primitive, or elaborate enough for a prince or a princess. You may want to have one handy, in a bedroom or perhaps in the living room, where guests who come bearing babies can rock them to sleep and not miss out on the conversation. After all, in the country everyone should be a part of things.

> "Here stood that trunk and here that chest,
> There lay that store I counted best."

So spoke Anne Bradstreet, one of the few women poets who wrote from the earliest years of our country. In her poem "Here Follows Some Verses Upon the Burning of Our House July 10, 1666," she mourns: "My pleasant things in ashes lie."

Because the closet was unknown to the early colonists, a family owned or made as many chests as it could manage and find room for. Bedding, linens, clothing—anything that needed protection from the air was put into chests. Later, dressers were added. Fortunately for the country decorator, choosing among them is a pleasure. Even the most humble of country chests will probably be more pleasing and better made than a modern one. What is a four-poster bed without a handsome New England maple chest of drawers? Chippendale, Queen Anne, Hepplewhite and Sheraton chests were as coveted in the eighteenth century as they are now. It's easy to understand why, once you've examined a few of these graceful pieces, with their fine, solid construction and meticulous attention to detail.

Of course the signed Chippendale or Sheraton piece is beyond the price range of all but a few, and those few would probably be nervous living with such priceless treasures. Fortunately, the "name" furniture makers of the past were so influential that many good copies were done by their contemporaries, and these pieces are available at more moderate prices. It's entirely possible to find a Chippendale-style chest with graceful fan-shaped curves or scrolled bracket feet that is well made, reasonably old, and affordable.

The Hepplewhite chest, popular around the end of the eighteenth century, is a simplified version of the Chippendale style. It too is well suited to a country bedroom: it has graceful curves, splayed legs, and scaled-down lines. Sheraton chests were a bit more pretentious as they tried to keep up with the Empire look that was all the rage in Europe. Sheraton pieces were hand-produced in the early nineteenth century and were popular all over the country. They are still honest and simple enough to fit well in a Down Home bedroom.

Blanket chests, another popular storage item, were meant to be placed at the foot of the bed. They are still a good height today for a cushioned seat. At the other end of the size extreme for storage was the enormous kas of the Netherlands. A kas can be a simple pine or a marvelously ornate mahogany or a walnut piece, carved, painted or stenciled. Definitely a dramatic piece of furniture, the kas should be given plenty of room in which to be appreciated.

Another kind of furniture, still in the wood category but unique in its way, is wicker. Wicker has been in everyone's good graces for so many years after its long exile in storage that you may overlook it when considering what country furniture to buy. Wicker is as natural to the country as baskets. What could look better on a porch or a sundeck, or in a windowed room facing a lake, than wicker, either plain or painted, with gleaming chintz cushions? Wicker belongs in any room: as a chair heaped with pillows on the back porch, as a settee in the hall, or as a chest in the bedroom. Because wicker has a light and airy look, it is well suited to small country rooms.

Country furniture is most plentiful and consequently cheaper in areas that were once affluent but are now in decline. People who live in real backwoods towns would probably *not* be shocked to hear what city slickers are paying for their "junk." Most country furniture dealers are aware of the value of things; but, still, they might just let you pick up something at a bargain because they want to make room for another estate, another nineteen rooms full of country furniture. . . .

It's highly unlikely that a country dealer will deliver your prize gentleman's chair or four-poster bed; so a station wagon, a van or a rental vehicle is a requirement for your furniture buying. But it's such a pleasure oing straight to the country for country things. Your good taste may some-  ay result in a cherished antique in the family—or it may not. Either way, e Down Home dweller is one who finds a wealth of enjoyment owning ces of the past: sitting on them, sleeping on them, and eating meals off ir fine old and slightly scarred wood finish.

*An English Bible box of the late 1500s rests here on a dark-stained English oak side table.*

*A pine gateleg table is a very rare find nowadays—even rarer than a tavern table. This one holds three Fulham salt-glaze tankards (circa 1720). The chair is a four-slat ladder-back in its original red paint. Note the added stretchers under the arms.*

Country chairs are available in all shapes and sizes, in many woods and in many paint colors. This group was photographed at Carousel Barn Antiques on Route 82 at Moore Mill, LaGrangeville, New York. The entire lot was priced at less than $100.

A round pine table is a useful piece for any room of the house. This one is set up for a checkers game. The seats of the side chairs have been hand-caned.

The Down Home country porch calls for Down Home rockers — and maybe even for metal chairs and a metal glider. On this porch, all the furniture has been painted deep green — a color that is always right for porch furniture.

Country furniture such as this combination blanket chest and two-drawer dresser is loved for every nick and worn spot. The original coat of red paint and its wooden knobs attest to the authenticity of this piece.

Often fashioned of a wood softer than pine, and not so slender in its turnings as the Windsor, the captain's chair has kept its popularity through the years, partly because it remains comfortable all through the after-dinner conversation.

*A hutch is essential to the Down Home kitchen or pantry also. When hutch shopping, select a piece with upper see-through glass doors for your family's treasured pitchers, goblets and plates.*

# Refinishing Old Country Wood

"Wood had a meaning and wood
  spoke to the feel of the fingers,
The hammer handles and the handwrought nails
  somehow had blessings."

*Carl Sandburg*
The People, Yes

For a country piece that needs restoring, the best advice is to do as little as possible. A chair that made it though the Civil War is not required to look like one that just came from the showroom. Cherish its nicks and bruises. (A one-hundred-year-old birdseye maple candle stand with a three-year-old cigarette burn on its surface is another matter, however.) If a piece is painted, it's best to leave it painted—unless the piece has the sparsest amount of carving or there is curly maple or rosy cherrywood under all the layers. And if it does not have some of these qualities, perhaps you should pass it up.

Approach your wood furnishings with respect. Treat wood gently. Don't dip it into a lye bath if a previous owner has painted it avocado and streaked it in umber with an antiquing kit. If its varnish is blistery and dark with age, or if its dirt has turned to a greasy smear over the years, there are less drastic procedures to try before you bring out the agents that eat through skin and

*he hand refinishing of woods such as these beautiful pieces
ngs joy and a sense of pride to the restorer, who is to be
gratulated for having been perceptive enough to see the
ity under the layers of ugliness.*

153

rubber gloves and will asphyxiate you unless you work with them in the open air.

Some enthusiasts attack old wood with shards of glass, razor blades, and sanders. It's hard to live with a piece of old wood that's been through all that. But don't despair. There are many steps between a simple cleaning with a damp rag and using a sanding belt. Here are some helpful measures that will restore your wood piece with a minimum of damage to restorer and restoree:

If you are very lucky, the piece you have bought is just dirty. You can hope that underneath fifty years of neglect is the original wax finish over the silvery oak, still intact. But that dirt may instead conceal a blistered, cracked or worn-through original finish. If all you have to do is to get down to the first finish, just rub the wood with a damp rag to remove the grime that is easily dissolved in water. Don't use detergent; it clouds a finish.

If after cleaning with a damp cloth you find that the original finish is still gritty, pour some paint thinner on a rag and rub all the surfaces again, using the thinner liberally. Then wipe dry. You may have restored your piece without disturbing its original finish, which is the most desired result; the original patina remains. Most important, the mellowing of age, the look that can never really be duplicated, has been retained in all its glory. Then you can apply a coat of wax or simply wipe the piece with an oil-based furniture polish and rub to a gloss. If you have been lucky enough to find a piece that still has its original stencils, this method will restore them best. Keep them preserved under a light coat of wax.

If the original finish is beyond the reach of paint thinner, you will need to determine, once your piece is wiped clean, the ingredients in the original finish. Two kinds of solvent will restore (not remove) most old varnish—lacquer thinner and denatured alcohol, the latter also called shellac thinner. Apply a bit of each to the underside to see which solvent works best to restore the original finish. Brush it on as if you were varnishing the piece. After the finish has thoroughly dried, rub it gently with a piece of fine steel wool. One solvent will not affect the varnish; the other will cause it to reamalgamate: that is, to adhere once more to the wood.

Then, using the solvent that works, brush it over the entire piece, let it dry thoroughly, and rub lightly with a fine grade of steel wool. Protect the surface with a thin coat of wax or an oil-based polish.

If there are too many coats of varnish on a piece, the reamalgamation method won't work. Nevertheless, do not run for the sander or lethal paint remover—yet. Mix the two solvents, lacquer thinner and denatured alcohol, in equal parts and cover the piece thickly with the mixture. Smear it around and then begin to wipe. Be prepared to remove endless amounts of smeary varnish. Apply more solvent, wipe, then apply and wipe again. In spite of the mess, this method is still preferable to disturbing the surface of the wood itself. A good refinisher opens up the pores of the wood only as a last resort (like a cosmetician who recommends dermabrasion only when all else fails). The application of the two solvents will also leave the stain intact, which is a plus. If you start removing stain, you have to remove it over the entire piece, which is difficult, because stain really sinks into pores.

Once you have removed all that sticky varnish and have rubbed your beautiful exposed wood with a fine steel wool pad, you can apply an old-fashioned paste wax. The result will be a patina that looks as old as the piece. If the original finish is not to your liking (perhaps the original stain is too dark and doesn't do justice to the interesting grain of the wood), rub household bleach into the surface with fine steel wool, using rubber gloves to protect your hands. Then wait twenty-four hours or until the piece is perfectly dry before applying a protective finish.

If you have bought a piece that has been painted sometime during its long history, don't scrape the surface looking for the birdseye or curly maple held in such low regard by our ancestors. Instead, prepare the surface as best you can and give it another coat of paint. Restoring it may well not be worth your time; and time is worth something, after all, even if it's vacation time.

The best way to paint a piece of wood furniture that has been nicked and kicked around in life is to give it several coats of primer and a final coat of good enamel. Trying to remove layers of paint from an ornately carved 1910 kitchen chair is a task for the masochist. You'll be sorry you ever started (and once you've started, you've got to finish). After all, the painted chair comes with the best of historical provenance: remember the Windsor chair, made up of so many different kinds of wood it was painted black and often stenciled to give it a uniform finish. So a painted chair is welcome in the best of Down Home rooms. If you don't like the typical enamel colors, try using a custom-mixed paint and several coats of varnish. Consult your paint store salesperson for particulars.

In spite of the warning above, let's say you have made a tiny scrape, found three birdseyes, and decided to restore your ugly-duckling blanket chest. Then wait until warm weather and do the job in the yard, using one of the popular paste paint removers. Smear it on thickly and cover with a sheet of dry cleaner's plastic. Let the chemicals work all night, and the following morning you will be shaving off a satisfyingly thick layer of blisters, underneath which you may well find another layer of paint.

Some paints come off handily when you smother them in a layer of toxic chemicals, but under them there may be two kinds of paint that won't budge. One is Victorian paint, usually applied with a fake wood grain. Leave it to the Victorians to cover up everything natural, even the finish of their wood! The leg they called limb, which you have so carefully exposed, you discover has a painted-on grain nearly as offending as the ersatz wood grain of Formica. Since most Down Home decorators feel that this kind of fakery is too ugly to be borne, you may want to paint the piece again—unless you proceed to the last resort, a sander. But wait. There is a second kind of paint that defies the modern paint remover. You just might have stumbled on a layer of milk paint, which is cause for rejoicing. Your pre-Civil War heart-backed chair really is what the dealer said it was if you find a milk paint finish, because widespread use of this homemade product eventually went out of style.

You can stop at this layer and leave the milk paint in all its tattered faded glory, or you can take the piece to its virgin wood condition. The latter is a case for the sander. Sanders will grind through veneers before you know it, but they also gouge and nick in the shaking hands of the amateur. Practice your technique on something less valuable before attempting a hand-sanding job on a country antique. A sander raises the nap of the wood, and your piece will require much diligent finishing, then a rubdown with a fine steel wool pad before it is ready for a finish. Some refinishing jobs are impossible for all but the driven maniac. Certain spool turnings are an example. This is one time when a trip through the lathe is the only practical way to remove a stubborn old finish.

Wood stripped to its virgin condition must be protected from air, heat, moisture, and especially dirt. If it is too light in color for your taste, stain it. The trouble with most commercial stains is their muddy quality. As with dyed hair, the nuances of shading are missing. The way to avoid the stain that goes on like paint is to use a transparent dye. It contains no pigment but truly stains the wood, sinking into the surface in varying degrees so that with careful wiping you can bring out differing tones in the wood. This way you will avoid a finished piece that is all one color, as indeed wood never is. Some furniture companies, particularly those that specialize in country reproduction, will sell you as little as a quart of commercial stain. Write to their customer service department.

The protective finish you use depends on the kind of wood, type of piece, and the look desired. A thin coat of wax can be burnished to a sheen, but varnish will give you a brighter shine. If what you want is a dull glow and you don't mind the furniture's darkening with age, you can apply an oil-based furniture polish.

If you varnish, seal the stain and any newly opened pores of the bare wood with shellac, then rub the surface with fine steel wool until it is as smooth as silk. Then apply several thin coats of varnish, rubbing to the same silky gloss between coats. A final rub with pumice and water or linseed oil will give you a truly professional finish.

Hand-refinished wood brings pride and joy to the restorer. You can congratulate yourself for having seen the beauty of a piece under its layers of ugliness and transforming it to its former glory. To be able to view such an object several times a day will have a restorative value in and of itself.

*Enjoy an old door for its beauty. Enjoy old hardware for its beauty too.*

*Approach the restoration of wood furnishings with respect. An old schoolroom desk should not be dipped into a lye bath, even if it has been painted over. There are many tricks to refinishing antique furnishings, and some should not be refinished at all.*

As evidence that finishes of quality survive, this English side table (circa 1650) still wears its original one. The carved heart decoration is an English piece.

# Country Collectibles

"Gentlemen, look on this wonder!
Whatever the bids of the bidders
   they cannot be high enough for it."
                                    *Walt Whitman*
                                    Leaves of Grass

The poet was prophetic, for any item Whitman may have seen on a nineteenth-century auction block is most certainly selling at a price that far exceeds the highest "bids of the bidders." The great joy of country collecting is that as one lives with an object of beauty, it steadily increases in value—and any assurance of future worth is a comfort in this age. A quality piece is thus better than money in the bank.

The word "antique" doesn't quite fit the country collectible. Antique implies high culture, fragility, museums. Nothing could be further from the truth of the Down Home collectible, which is quite simply something old and well designed that serves a function, whether it is a Shaker rug, a railroad lamp, or a tulip-patterned goblet. The joy of country collecting is in the using, and in the process of collecting you will learn much not only about art but about history.

*Dutch pewter plates and utensils are displayed on a Dutch plate rack. The dried breads from various European countries are collectibles too.*

Willowware, candle stands, fire screens, applique quilts, boot scrapers, mercury glass, coffee mills, cooky cutters, backyard benches and weathervanes—there are uses for all functional country antiques both within and without the house.

The kitchen is a favorite place to display and use your treasures. Grind coffee in your big cheerful country store coffee mill instead of turning it into a lamp or a plant holder. Jugtown pottery or Bennington jugs are beautiful on display, but they should be handy enough to use—carefully. Fat oval noodle boards, pudding steamers, ventilated pie safes, heart-shaped waffle irons, treenware, balance scales, flatirons and stands, flapjack shovels, painted tin matchboxes, pastry wheels—the list is virtually endless. Many old pieces work better than their modern counterparts, and some treasures rival the whimsy of Calder's kitchen objects. Display them openly and use them for special occasions to keep them real objects rather than *objets d'art*.

Treenware is a favorite collectible. "Treen" is plural for tree in old English, an appropriate word for a wooden object. Pine, maple, oak and walnut are among the most popular woods used in making these simple pieces of kitchenware that have aged so well. Along with the more common spoons, ladles and cups, there are carved treen springerle rolling pins, lemon squeezers, sand shakers, maple sugar molds—a long list of objects, from the practical to the whimsical.

Many a country family threw out its mundane treenware and even its dented pewter when the tinker came through town selling his shiny new ware. Tinware, known as "poor man's silver," was made out of sheet iron coated with a layer of molten tin to prevent rusting and was sold around the countryside by itinerant peddlers. Tinware was popular not only for its shine, but also for its practicality and comparatively low price. When tinware was painted with designs it was called toleware, a highly popular decorative style in the Colonies. The Pennsylvania Germans also loved to paint tin with their cheerful motifs. From cake molds to washbasins, chandeliers to pudding steamers, much tinware still exists, whether painted or shiny, that has good design as well as function.

Most country metalware should have a modest sheen to it—the glow of copper, pewter and brass rather than the rich gleam of silver. The ornate silver designs of the King's Men is really not appropriate to Down Home décor. The clean and simple designs of Paul Revere and his imitators, the works of American metalsmiths, were usually much simpler than those of the European. Opulence and splendor didn't spread to the rural areas of the

New World, and for the most part ornate silver tea sets, gleaming bowls and pitchers richly encrusted with raised rosettes and ormolu are simply not going to blend in with the forthright Down Home style.

The dining room hutch is a favorite place to display a precious collection of Liverpool transfer-printed china or Sgraffito. Our Victorian ancestors loved fancy pressed glass, rooster-and-hen-covered serving dishes, mochaware, blown glass decanters, ironstone, and goblets. Much of it still has appeal today. Pressed glass is especially popular; look for it in pineapple, bull's eye or sawtooth design. Finely etched, delicate Fostoria glassware is another favorite, perfect for high feast days like Thanksgiving and Christmas. Some people like to collect antique china dinnerware piece by piece and couldn't care less whether plates or cups match. Others can't resist buying whole cupboards full of the ever popular blue and white willowware.

Living rooms can be one hundred percent collectible, from the andirons to the hooked rug to the pewter chandelier fitted with fat white candles. Or they can be a mixture of styles. Our thrifty ancestors didn't believe in discarding the old to make room for the new, and they too lived with period mixtures. A grandfather clock goes well with a traditional sofa, to say nothing of a candle stand, a baptismal certificate, or a row of decoy ducks with glass eyes—so long as each piece is of good design.

Country collectibles are also at home on the living room wall. Portraiture is a favorite. If your ancestors didn't leave you their portraits, adopt a cou-

*Iron pots, iron pots everywhere! Iron pots such as these hung above many a fire in the early colonist's home. Iron pots have become popular collectibles, and their value is increasing at a rapid pace.*

ple. True portrait collectors cannot bear to break up a man and wife, and many a pair look down on a country living room.

The charm of country portraiture lies not in the fulfillment of dynastic pretensions but in the love of the past made tangible. Many portrait lovers speak of the "good karma" of having a sober face with merry eyes looking down on the present from the past. Whether your ancestor portrait is actually great-great-grandmother or a country auction find with a haunting resemblance to *someone* in your family, there is something very satisfying about living with old pictures.

Another favorite collectible is the fruit-and-flower motif of "theorem" painting, which was done on velvet, usually white, in the early nineteenth century. Although the diversion was short-lived, it was widespread. Cultured young ladies bored with needlework enjoyed the novelty of painting on velvet; and, since the painting was done by stencil, the task required more patience and care than artistic ability. The stencils, or "theorems," were applied color by color, as many as the artist could manage with a steady meticulous stroke. Paintings on velvet found today are mostly museum pieces, but the art has been revived and practiced at such places as Old Sturbridge in Massachusetts. Look for quality contemporary pieces, especially if you are a lover of Victorian flower-and-fruit motifs.

*Papier mâché* was the molded plastic of the nineteenth century. A mash of paper and glue was molded, smoothed, then painted and varnished into everything from George Washington's ceiling panels to mother-of-pearl-inlaid snuffboxes. It was also commonly lacquered to look as though it had come from the Orient. Sewing boxes, vases, even clocks were popular items of *papier mâché*, and they continue to be esthetically pleasing in a Down Home setting.

Folk Art is a label applied to a style of ornamental country decor that has its roots deep in the Old World. No matter how hard and dreary one's life, it is the nature of the human being to brighten up that life with cheerful design and color. Like most country folk, our American forebears weren't trained in art, but they were clever with their hands, accustomed as they were to creating nearly everything they needed at home. If they couldn't afford the price of imported *papier mâché* or stenciled tin trays, folk artists created plenty of their own designs, as old as memory, with which they decorated their homes. The style is often called "primitive," and it's true that most country folk had not studied perspective or did not know that common objects were not then considered appropriate subjects for art. That's what makes folk art so appealing: its naturalness and exuberance—lacking the restraints that high culture put on art.

From Germany, Switzerland, France, the British Isles, Scandinavia and Russia, peasants came to America with a variety of decorating traditions that went back to the Middle Ages. The best known today, of course, is the cheerful folk art of the Pennsylvania Dutch. These settlers weren't Dutch at all; the word for German, *Deutsch*, was mispronounced and the label stuck. The light-hearted designs so familiar to Americans include tulips and other flowers, hearts, and hexes on barns. Nearly every mundane object, from dough boxes to tin coffeepots, was ornamented. It was the Germans who brought over to Pennsylvania certain customs pertaining to childhood that soon became such a part of the new American tradition. Without the Pennsylvania "Deutsch," we might have no Christmas tree, Santa or Easter bunny.

In the rich Pennsylvania farmland of their new home, these country folk prospered. Their gay motifs have been reproduced to the point that many people find them tiresome, but a look at authentic Pennsylvania folk art will revive the interest of all but the most jaded.

Each symbol has a meaning. The heart symbolizes love for both God and humanity. The tulip, with its three stylized petals, represents the Trinity. Even the birds have significance: the dove for peace, the peacock for heaven. The familiar hex signs date back to those terrible years when the Church in Old and New World alike set out to destroy all vestiges of pagan culture, particularly those in which women had special powers. The folk artist turned this dark side of human nature, witch-hunting, into something cheerful. The Pennsylvania Dutch hex sign doesn't look like a spell to keep witches away. There is nothing sinister about the star, the circle, or the flower symbols used in the typical hex, but the symbols did have meaning that went deep into history, long before the Christian era. The whorl was the ancient symbol of the duality of nature, good and evil, yin and yang; the star a symbol of the sun; the flower of eternal life.

With these so-called pagan symbols, the Pennsylvania Dutch kept witches away from their fat, full barns. Hexes have been painted on barns and other objects of folk art for so long that their original intent has been forgotten by many. Few sights are more pleasing then a big Pennsylvania barn with its sturdy stone foundation and a rich and colorful hex symbol fore and aft.

*Fractur* is another coveted folk art, so rare that most of it is safely tucked away in museums. This form of ornamented calligraphy looks like an il-

Ruth Davis at the Greenbrier Hotel Arts Colony makes new Christmas tree collectibles of straw and felt. Her Mr. and Mrs. Santa Claus have decorated my own country tree. And here is Ruth's Christmas Angel, made from straw and acorns.

luminated manuscript penned by a Pennsylvania folk artist—which it often was. The ornate lettering, intertwined with swirls, flowers, birds, vines laden with grapes, and other common motifs of the illuminated religious manuscript, was employed by the folk artist in family documents which were then framed and hung on the wall. These gaily painted marriage, birth or baptismal certificates commemorated happy events, as did *"Haus-segen,"* or house blessings. Although so rare that it is not truly a collectible, at least not in the price range of the majority of collectors, *fractur* is something the collector of early Americana should know about.

To the Pennsylvania Dutch we owe some of the most pleasing of Down Home features—the rocking chair, the Dutch door, the expanded window, and color all around. From furniture to glassware to the lavishly ornamented dower chest, Pennsylvania folk art can brighten up every corner of your house.

The Scandinavians brought over a unique form of folk art called rosemaling. Its fruit-and-flower motif was executed free-hand, and many cracked immigrant chests with faded rosemaling and peeling Gothic lettering have been lovingly passed from generation to generation. Unlike stenciling, free-hand rosemaling requires considerable skill. Favorite colors are russet red, ice blue, dark orange, and jade green—muted hues rather than the bright primary color schemes of other kinds of folk art. The colors were muted further still by several coats of varnish, for in most Scandinavian households all the furniture was varnished once a year. As a consequence, many pieces of rosemaling may need the skill of the extremely careful restorer.

Like so many folk arts, rosemaling is being revived around the country. If you can't find a good contemporary example, learn to do it yourself!

Precious vestiges of old transplanted cultures that managed to escape the American melting pot, folk art is truly "of the people, by the people and for the people."

More collectibles: the list of functional pieces is endless, the varieties wide and tempting. Clocks and mirrors are two more for you to consider. Every country home had to have a clock, and since these pieces were usually treated with care, many have survived in working order. To many Down Homers, the muted ticktock of a pendulum clock and its occasional gentle chiming are as essential to the atmosphere as the smell of gingerbread. The undisputed favorite is the grandfather clock, the kind that stood on the floor and "stopped, short, never to go again when the old man died." Fortunately, most antique grandfather clocks are not so loyal, and their quality inner workings can often easily be repaired.

But there are other kinds of clocks to suit individual fancies. Grandmother clocks also stand on the floor but are shorter than the grandfather variety, and there are bracket clocks that hang on a wall, eight-day calendar clocks, lyre-shaped mantel clocks, wagon clocks, banjo, pillar-and-scroll, steeple-on-steeple, and fancy paint-and-gilt Victorian clocks. Pendulum clocks chime and tick too loudly for some, but for many lovers of the country life, the sounds are reminiscent of happy childhood hours. Whatever your preference, a country house must have a timepiece. Why not invest in the real thing?

A house must also have mirrors. Most people would not want to install wall-to-wall mirrors in a country home, but they might use antique mirrors to help open up a room, reflect an object of beauty, or simply hang in the hall or bathroom for peering into. The choices run the gamut of country styles, from simple Federal to graceful Hepplewhite to ornate Victorian painted cast-iron.

And what is a country house without some toys? Children must also have their playthings. Cradles are a favorite collectible. In the city they are often filled with magazines, but in the country they look wonderful filled with dolls. From a Civil War era "Mammy" doll (for looking) to a 1940s Betsey-Wetsey doll (for gentle playing), a cradle full of dolls will appeal to people of any age. Until the late nineteenth century, there were no American doll manufacturers, but many enthusiasts are collecting twentieth-century dolls which they hope will potentially become valuable antiques. Rag dolls, Waterbury walking dolls, wax dolls, dolls with delicate china faces and eyes of sapphire blue, adult dolls—replicas of famous contemporary actresses or miniature mannequins wearing the latest fashion—the field is wide open. From a decorating standpoint, antique dolls can't go wrong—especially in the country.

A rocking horse is another sure winner. In the city, antique rocking horses are sometimes fastened to the wall with downlights overhead. In the country they look better on the floor, waiting for a child.

Doll furniture runs a close third to dolls and rocking horses, and the opportunities for collectors are good, since Victorians were wild about miniatures. Playing with dollhouses is another childhood pastime whose fascination extends into adulthood.

Toy collecting in general is a lot of fun. Mechanical banks can be most amusing: fat Tammany Hall politicians deposit coins in an inner pocket, puppies wag their tails in response to a deposit, frogs roll their eyes and gulp down money. Some toy collectors concentrate on a single category, like locomotives, boats or carved animals. Others take an eclectic approach and buy whatever appeals to them. A toy collection (behind glass if it's an investment) is a success not just in a child's bedroom but also in the hall, the living room, family room—or any Down Home room, for that matter.

Collectibles aren't confined to the interior, however. Much living went on outside the house in the past, and so objects created for outside use have also become sought-after country collectibles. Sleighs, oxbows, sleds, grain boxes, winnowing scoops, cobbler's benches, washtubs and other large containers are all farmyard objects that can be functional as well as pleasing to the eye. However, collectors aren't limited to the farmyard. Tavern signs—bearing eagles, whaling ships or the word "liberty"—are highly popular, as are mileposts, weathervanes, ship's lanterns, outdoor cooking utensils, mailboxes and old gates. (The latter are now so popular that Down Home people are often called to the door by passing strangers asking whether they will sell the gate to their frontyard. The attitude of the collector is, "You never know—they might.")

Weathervanes are a particularly pleasing combination of form and function. Horses, fish, birds, mermaids, ships, sea serpents, angels, and of course eagles all indicated the wind direction—and that was an important function in those days. Unless your treasured weathervane is fragile with age, why not use it as such rather than turning it into a mobile?

Nearly everything functional in Victorian times was gussied up, and some of the results are now valuable for curiosity's sake if for no other. Even the lowly foot scraper of that age was ornamented with a lyre or scroll design, and the bootjack was even more ornate. A popular shape was the beetle-and-lyre, with the antenna serving as a V-shaped clamp to grasp the shoe heel for easy removal of the boot. Other popular shapes were pistols, crickets, and something naughty called "Nellie." If you find yourself enamored of foot scrapers and bootjacks, why not honor their traditional use? You'll have an amusing history lesson at your very door.

Of course, reproductions of many of the collectibles in this chapter are available, but the sad truth about reproductions is they never really make it. Something old has a look, a feel, an aura of history about it that something new can never have. And since reproductions can cost as much or even more than the real thing (in some instances, two reproductions cost as much as one real thing), why buy something of dubious value? An imitation grandfather clock, no matter how artfully distressed, will still look new—as do reproduction Jenny Lind desks, Tiffany-style lampshades, and those popular gleaming brass fixtures with three balls. In the city, reproductions can fit into a certain artificiality of style, but in the country they're as out of place as a bouquet of plastic daisies.

Many people find it fun to fortune-hunt on weekends in the country, where auctions, flea markets, antique stores and yard or garage sales abound. The best place to buy collectibles is in a once-affluent area where people bought nice things their descendants now want to sell, whether by choice or of necessity.

Once you're hooked, bone up on country collectibles. Many good books and periodicals are available in bookstores and libraries. When you're ready to go treasure hunting, plan to buy the best pieces you can afford—one good item is better than three items of lesser value—and concentrate on those that have a function along with a pleasing form. If you buy something, try to honor its original function, but if you can't, don't worry about it. No one boils shirts over an open fire anymore, but antique washboilers are perfect for steaming a big batch of clams or cooking pasta for twenty.

Above all, collect with an activated sense memory. Look for things you remember from your own past, or for things that vaguely remind you of pleasant moments . . . drinking Grandma's lemonade out of a pineapple pressed glass goblet, or swinging on her American flag gate. Collectibles are of value because they honor the past. Don't neglect to honor your own.

*Barbra Streisand is a collector. This antique circus wagon and horse sit on the floor under a black baby grand piano in the actress's New York apartment.*

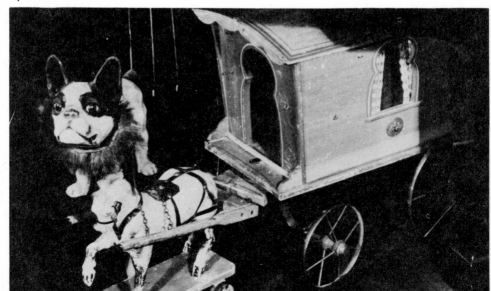

*Salt-glaze pitchers are displayed on the top shelf in this country kitchen. On the second shelf are pieces of historic Staffordshire and some Bennington ware. On the bottom— an antique dollhouse and a spongeware bowl.*

There's a bit of everything in this collectible closet: pieces of treen; soft paste, a kind of early pottery; pewter; and on the fourth shelf down, a collection of antique silhouettes.

Miniature English houses made of clay can be purchased all over Great Britain. This group of new houses is displayed on wood shelving in the library of an English home in the American Midwest.

Today's makers of collectibles—such as potter Paul Chaleff—work in clay in rural America. These photographs were taken at Stissing Mountain Craftsmen, Pine Plains, New York. Mr. Chaleff's ceramics have graced the homes of America's finest collectors of New Down Home—and his pieces have decorated the tables in our White House too!

On this antique brick wall a collection of wooden spoons hangs alongside a Dutch wooden shoe. The antique wooden shelf holds a group of interesting jars.

A collection of round blue and white dot stands decorate a hanging Queen Anne shelf of English oak. The round pieces were bases for teapots. The square plaques are blue and white tiles.

*Bean pots and old crockery make great collectibles. If you happen across some crockery at a country auction, buy if the price is right. I believe bean pots will increase in value in the coming years.*

*Fill an old wooden crib with wine bottles and crystal glass. This is just one of the interesting ways to use old furnishings in today's world of Down Home decorating.*

# Baskets

"Leaving me baskets covered with white towels, swelling the house with their plenty," wrote America's nineteenth-century bard Walt Whitman. He wrote his ode to baskets in the epic poem *Leaves of Grass*, an appropriate work for the subject of baskets. Aside from leaves like the flat and sinewy palmetto or grasses so fine they can be braided, the basket maker also uses many other natural materials.

Willow rods, peeled or unpeeled; honeysuckle vine, roots, bark, twigs, pine needles . . . for thousands of years, the basket has been an essential carrier, and in the New World the ancient basketry of the Indians merged with the ancient basketry methods of the Old. The result is a uniquely American basket, a treasure to own as well as to use.

The American Indians used over one hundred different kinds of natural materials, selecting them for color, dimension, strength, and flexibility to

*Owning one of the many antique baskets is like living with a bit of history. Baskets hung from the ceiling bring charm to this American country herb house.*

make their extraordinary geometrically patterned basketry which sometimes employed circular patterns within the geometrics. Indians, being mostly nomadic, needed many baskets. They made them for ritual as well as for everyday use for the shaman, the hunter, and the gatherer. Covered creels were made for the fisher, pack baskets for horses and dogs, and pouch-shaped baskets for children to gather nuts or bits of wood from bushes. Baskets were also used for serving food hot from the fire.

Brightly colored feathers, shells and beads were sometimes woven into ritual baskets. The Apaches made music with baskets that were fringed with strips of leather, a bell at the end of each strip. They also made objects of beauty that were used to house steaming pots, or to bring home leftovers, or to sift corn in.

From California to the Bering Straits, native Americans spent the long, cold, wet rainy season indoors. Lewis and Clark described a typical winter-ing in what is now coastal Washington State that captures the wet dreariness of those months. Indians passed the time indoors making baskets. Practice made perfect: some of the baskets of these Northwestern tribes are pricelessly beautiful. They were often made of cedar bark, coiled rather than woven in and out of a rib, and look magnificent today, whether used as a centerpiece to hold fruit and nuts or skeins of yarn, or hanging on the wall ready for gathering flowers or herbs.

The Indians of the Southwest, nomadic and home dwellers alike, made baskets for trade. They used the kinds of vegetation that grow in arid soil, such as yucca leaf, willow rod and coarse grasses. Their baskets, neatly coiled geometric wonders of stars and arrows, are still being made today by local native Americans, and in fact are an important part of their economy. Owning one of these baskets is like living with a bit of history.

The Choctaw, Cherokee, Seminole and Chitimacha all had their own basketry techniques. The tribes around the Great Lakes used a distinctive twist in their weaving called *curlicue*. They hand-painted their baskets, or stenciled designs of wolves or other animal totems on their ritual vessels. The Indians of the Northeast braided finely textured sweet grass coils into beautiful baskets, and also made sturdier ones of smooth honeysuckle vine.

The Gulla tribe of South Carolina was the one most influenced by the foreign cultures. Their basketry has a strong African look to it; many baskets are of coiled sweet grass with strips of palmetto and pine needles used for a contrasting stripe in the overall design.

It would seem that the American Indian did not know how to make anything utilitarian that was not also a thing of beauty. No wonder collecting Indian basketry is so popular. From Maine to New Mexico, from the Bering Straits to Florida, you will find local Indian basketry craft well worth learning about.

Many of America's immigrants brought with them basketry skills learned in the old country—especially the German settlers in Pennsylvania—but they were also influenced by the Indians' craft. Like so many works of utilitarian art at cultural crossroads, a new type of basket—a blending of both worlds—arose. It is uniquely American, and the best examples are already national treasures.

Some of the most treasured are the Shaker pieces. This religious sect earned its nickname because its adherents were Quakers who quite literally shook during their rituals—the only flamboyant thing about them. The Shakers practiced an esthetic creed of utility in all things. Everything they made had to have a useful purpose, and no unnecessary adornment was allowed. But as it always will, beauty found its way into the objects these devout people made, and a Shaker hamper, kitchen storage basket or openwork cheese curd drainer can be a work of art and should be treated as such. Surely no one will want to use a curd drainer for making cheese, but it would look wonderful by the fireplace, holding a sheaf of oats at harvest time. The Shaker basket is one in which the Indian influence is evident. Some of the most desirable baskets are the heavy-duty kind, made with wood splints, which would have held enough lunch for a family of twelve in the churchyard.

The Pennsylvania Germans used the coiled rye straw basket for many of their functions; they even made baskets to cover their beehives in the wintertime.

Sailors also made baskets; the Nantucket lightship basket is now a collector's prize. While on duty in the lightships that served as nautical lighthouses in another era, the sailors wove these rattan baskets with movable handles, often nesting them inside each other to take up less space.

In Appalachia one can find baskets named "melon" or "Granny's fanny," after their shapes. The construction is ribbed; unpeeled willow rods are used in a design that often culminates in a beautiful diamond-shaped pattern around the handles. Another favorite is the Carolina basket, with sides curving up to meet overhead in an O-shaped handle.

Long before paper bags, shopping bags, plastic bags, cardboard boxes and closets, the basket was used for everything from holding a trinket to toting a hundred pounds of potatoes, from plucking a goose to carrying a baby. If you love baskets and want to use them in your home, the various sizes, shapes and patterns are legion. Honor their original use, or find new uses for the different shapes. Here are some traditional basket uses. Egg baskets were often shaped like an oriole's nest, and sometimes held exact dozens. Potatoes, apples and turnips were gathered in baskets so heavy and strong that they could hold up under as much as a hundred pounds. They were made with two handles, so they could be transported by two people or could be tied to the waist. Finely woven baskets were used for sowing seed or were made in a fan shape for winnowing. Cheese baskets had an openwork weave that would allow cheese to drain. Similar openweave baskets were used for drying fruit or herbs because the air could circulate freely.

Lined with a blanket, a basket was a portable cradle. Covered with a cloth, it was a gift box. And for a holiday function, it could hold two pies, the second on an inner shelf with legs. But there were dozens of more mundane uses—draining the wash, raising dough, holding kindling. Baskets were also used when cutting flowers, for holding the mail or skeins of yarn, for mending, or for bringing home trout, berries or mushrooms. They were put to work in the dairy, the barnyard, the pantry, the henhouse, the porch, upstairs and downstairs, and in the root cellar.

Today, baskets have a hundred other uses that didn't exist even a couple of generations ago. But one thing a basket should not be is strictly for show. In the country, touches must be authentic or they stand out at once and declare themselves a "decorator's statement." Country harvest displays in chic stores, with baskets overhead, price tags aflutter, are trying to duplicate a look; but those baskets will have to be put to good use or they will lack that Down Home quality of utilitarian beauty.

*This antique basket from Alsace, France, was used for gathering grapes. In our history, baskets have been used for everything from holding a trinket to toting a hundred pounds of potatoes; from plucking a goose to carrying a baby.*

*For thousands of years the basket has been an essential carrier. For collectors the ancient basketry of the Indians of the New World has merged with the ancient basketry methods of the Old.*

A Trug basket (from Sussex, England) can serve as a bird feeder. Try hanging one on a stick in your rose garden, close to the stone wall.

An unusual bird feeder (this one made in Devon, England) can lend bucolic charm to any country garden.

# Country Fireplaces

"You can always see a face in the fire."
*Henry David Thoreau*
Walden

Home fires create far more than warmth. The fireplace has played a central role in our country's literature; it has been referred to so often that one can almost see whole generations of Americans cozying up not only for warmth, of course, but also for inspiration, for comfort, for contemplation. . . .

To gather around a roaring fire while outside one's dwelling the elements rattle and shake is surely one of man's oldest satisfactions. It's obvious to anyone who has ever had a fireplace that people *need* to spend time around one; a country house without this ancient source of pleasure will not truly satisfy. If you have room for only one major improvement or addition to your country house, put your money into a fireplace.

If you already have one, this chapter will give you ideas for how to make the most of it. If your country house is sadly without, this chapter will help you plan for what is lacking. If you *do* add a fireplace, you'll of course be in-

*The large stone fireplace is favored by many Down Homers. The mantel above the wide opening in this one holds tin candle molds, crockery, samplers, and a variety of country antiques.*

creasing the value of your property. And think of the energy crisis. . . .

"Every man looks at his wood-pile with a kind of
affection. I love to have mine before my window . . ."

*Henry David Thoreau*
Walden

Wood is a renewable energy source; petroleum and coal are not. While we wait for the new solar technologies to become economically viable heating alternatives, it pays to install a fireplace. As the cost of fossil fuels spirals ever upward, you too will look on your woodpile with affection!

An indoor source of heat is essentially no more than an enclosure of metal or stone, a fire, and a funnel to carry off smoke and fumes, whether it's an igloo with a hole in its roof or a clanking, roaring octopus of a boiler in the basement. With the advent of central heating and the use of fossil fuels, the source of warmth moved to the basement, where people were rarely motivated to pull up chairs and sip cider. Over the years, it became virtually invisible: a heating coil behind the draperies, a discreet register, or a covered-up radiator. Fortunately, the charm and solace of the open fire are still within the realm of possibility, even if your country home was built during those years when people were glad to live without "messy, smoky" fireplaces.

### Enclosures

The earliest indoor fire was the central open hearth, and such an arrangement continues to have its appeal. These first hearths, like some of today's innovations, were often elevated. The advantages of a centrally located fire are obvious: maximum radiation on every side, plus the possibility of multiple usage. Some of the country homes were built with a central hearth, but it took up a great deal of space, and so a wall location was usually preferred to make maximum use of a small area. If you want a central hearth and don't have the good fortune to live in a house that has one, there is an alternative in one of the many varieties of freestanding fireplace stoves.

The prebuilt freestanding fireplace comes fully equipped with hearth, hood, pipe, and all the fixings. A hood is often essential for a freestanding fireplace because a fire that is open on all sides tends to smoke without optimum draft conditions. Fortunately, hoods that range in style and price from inexpensive sheet metal to gleaming copper can add a dramatic touch to a central fireplace as well as reflect additional heat. These central fireplaces are ideal for homes designed with wide-open spaces—some A-frames, for instance, and converted barns. Since the energy crisis of the mid-1970s, prebuilt fireplaces are also available with heat-circulating systems that increase their efficiency.

But the home decorator need not be limited to new central fireplaces. Antique varieties are perhaps even more pleasing. The Franklin stove, with its removable door to expose the roaring fire inside, has always been a great favorite. Decorative cast iron was also popular for a long time. The great advantage of the freestanding stove is that it can be placed in any of a variety of locations, provided its pipe will reach an outside wall. Some of the wedding-cake stoves with fancy trimmings are more than conversation pieces: they are also excellent auxiliary sources of heat. Many have such added advantages as interchangeable drafts and loading doors, stovepipes that also function as radiators, and elaborate vases that hold water to humidify the room. When people started building two-story houses, fireplaces were moved from the central hearth to the wall. Eventually they were built into the wall and given a chimney and a separate flue for each opening. This is the kind of fireplace that most country dwellers think of when they envision chestnuts roasting.

> "The mug of cider simmered slow,
> the apples sputtered in a row,
> and, close at hand, the basket stood
> with nuts from brown October's wood."
>
> *John Greenleaf Whittier*
> Snowbound

The masonry fireplace that serves for both cooking and warmth is the type of fireplace that for many centuries people sat around, baked their food in and even slept on top of. But before you set your heart on something so massive, consider your needs. An enormous fireplace may overheat a small room. An enormous fireplace with a small fire, on the other hand, may not heat a room efficiently at all. The laws of thermodynamics should govern the size of the opening of a fireplace. The heat comes not so much from the flame itself but from the radiation sent out by the surrounding brick or ironwork. If the opening is too large, the walls will not be close enough to the heat source for this radiation to be effective, and much of the heat will be dissipated. Consult an expert before installing or renovating a really big fireplace.

If you are planning to have a fireplace built into one of the walls of your home, why not consider something a little different while you're about it? A corner fireplace, for instance, whether on an inside or an outside wall, is especially cozy. Then there is the ultimate room divider: a two-way fireplace with double the heat and double the pleasure. The two-way fireplace is ideal for planners who would like to have an open fire in their kitchen as well as in their living/dining area. There are even three-way fireplaces, built like peninsulas, with one side accommodating a grill. Before you start drawing up plans, however, consult a heating expert; a multiple fireplace enclosure presents special cross-draft problems. Another important consideration is the placement of doors. You won't want a fireplace wedged in between two doors, since you'd then have the problem of people trafficking through your reveries.

Most of all, consider space. You need enough room around a wall fireplace for people to sit comfortably. If you plan to use your fireplace for cooking, too, provide space for utensils. Nothing is more frustrating than realizing that you have failed to consider such a simple thing as a cooking space at the proper height when drawing up plans that don't allow for any retro-fitting. This is one of the reasons a corner fireplace can be so successful—the entire area can be used for cooking or just plain sitting without being in the middle of the action.

*If you don't have a real live one to sit on the hearthside rug, why not consider a cast iron cat?*

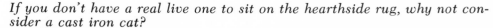

## The Fireplace Wall

If you like a masonry facing, materials for it might be lying right out there in your own pasture. Think of brick taking on the fire's rosy glow . . . it has lots of character and may even make the fireplace look as if it had always been there. Sometimes wood is combined with brick on a fireplace wall. (Check local regulations regarding the distance required between a flammable material and the fireplace opening.) If you yearn for the roseate and rustic look of the roaring fire in historical or museum rooms of early Americana, consider a heavy slab of wood, flush with the masonry facing if you like, as a lintel. Another Colonial favorite is wood paneling, which can be installed with neat moldings on the entire fireplace wall.

Ceramic tile is also popular. Delft is a natural in a Pennsylvania Dutch setting, and Spanish tile is just as natural to the Southwestern country home. Your fireplace can be the focal point of a room. Lavish thought upon it.

## Mantels

The traditional purpose of the mantel was to serve as a handy shelf for keeping food warm, so a kitchen fireplace should have one. Mantels also mask the opening of a fireplace and give the wall a finished look. Like everything country, mantels are a widely disparate lot. There are smooth marble ones, ornate plaster ones, clean and simple Adam and classic Georgian mantels, fancy cast iron mantels and mantels made of plain, rugged wood. Victorian mantels are a little more restrained than most furnishings in that style, although some are predictably excessive. Shopping for the right mantel is one of the pleasures of furnishing your fireside. Try to see a large assortment before you choose, as the mantel should serve as a pedestal for some of the things you cherish most. Whatever makes you happiest to look upon, if it befits a mantel, display it there. It may be a carved wood decoy, or a pair of pewter candlesticks, or family photographs, or several porcelain pieces. Whatever you put there, make it special.

Above the mantel is another special place. One carefully selected painting often works better than several, especially if the colors in the painting ignite when logs are burning. Or you might want to use a mirror in an interesting frame. During the warm season, flowers and plants are a natural on the mantel as well as in the fireplace opening. There, you might also try using a large and showy mass of rhododendron leaves, or sheaves of grain, in a generous container of wood, ceramic or metal.

The hearth itself in front of the fire must be made of noncombustible materials to prevent flying sparks from landing on varnished wood or precious rugs and furniture. A fire in the house is a serious responsibility; fire screens are always a good safeguard.

If you are thinking of installing a fireplace, why not consider a raised or cantilevered hearth? With a handy stack of pillows, the raised hearth is ideal for seating a number of people comfortably around the fire.

The hearth is also the spot where tools for tending the fire should be kept at the ready, as well as a container for logs—all the accoutrements of the well-built and well-kept fire. There is an English joke about the insufferable guest who stoked his host's fire even though he'd scarcely known him for seven years. Since Americans are less concerned about the prerogatives of owner-ship, you should stock the country hearth with whatever a person needs—homeowner and guest alike—to participate in the pleasure of building and tending a fire. Decorating the hearth is another opportunity to combine function and beauty, for there is an abundance of accessories for sale.

Andirons are one of those items that brought out the fancy in the crafts-people who made them. The andiron's original use was to hold a spit for roasting food over the flame. Today's andiron is likely to be more decorative than functional, but who can resist a pair of Hessian soldiers condemned to the hearthside flames—a favorite type of andiron in fledgling America. How the new citizens must have enjoyed putting these symbols of the hated mercenaries where they would receive their just reward.

Andirons are made plain or fancy in handsome brass or wrought iron. The brass ones with urn- or bell-shaped finials are impressive, even if they no longer suspend the suckling pig.

The fire screen is another important hearthside accessory. The types most people know today are the fireproof mesh and the one of tempered glass which some people object to because it masks the feeling of the open fire. But there is another type of fire screen which was originally intended to keep the glare of the fire out of the person's eyes—in past years, people must have been more sensitive to light than we are in these days of overlit rooms. In any event, you may find an irresistible fire screen on a pedestal, executed in needlework or painted with birds, flowers or cornucopias, that will enhance your center-of-attraction even more.

A receptacle for holding wood or coal is another chance for you to com-bine function and beauty. Consider gleaming copper or brass, a wood or ceramic tub, open metalwork or basketry. Look for such a carrier and you

*The old-brick facing on the fireplace gives it the true country look. The simple mouldings around the hearth are appropriate to the Down Home style.*

will find it: as soon as you start thinking in terms of something round, substantial and pleasing to the eye, you are likely to stumble across some perfectly ingenious fuel carrier that is uniquely your style.

While you're looking for the perfect fuel receptacle, keep your eye out too for pokers, tongs, shovels and brushes. There's no rule that says they have to be a matching set. They are sure to be more interesting if they are acquired piece by piece.

**The Fire**

> "A few pieces of fat pine were a great
> treasure. . . . Commonly I kindled my fire on the dry
> leaves of the forest, which I had stored up in my
> shed before the snow came. Green hickory finely
> split makes the woodchopper's kindling."
>
> 

*Henry David Thoreau*
Walden

The fireplace lover quickly develops preferences in the kinds of wood he uses. Some woods burn with a pleasing fragrance. Thoreau's few pieces of fat pine were a great treasure because well-cured pine snaps and crackles merrily as its pockets of pitch ignite and turn to gas. (Such a fire also sputters, so a closed fire screen is a good idea.) Apple, hickory and eucalyptus woods all have a distinctive aroma, as does pine. Woods burn in different colors too. Near the seashore, country dwellers can have driftwood fires of startling blue and pale purple.

But wood isn't the only fuel that works well in a country fireplace. You can also experiment with coal and charcoal, particularly if some cooking goes on in your fireplace. Just be sure you don't use coal that has been soaked in a flammable liquid, or scrap wood that has been painted or varnished: toxic fumes would fill your room.

Now for the final act: the fire itself. One of the most important design schemes in the country dwelling is the arrangement of logs for a blazing fire. It was a fine old English custom to have servants standing by each fireplace, matches at the ready, as guests came up the drive. The wintertime welcome of a rosy fire is one of the greatest of human joys. It deserves a paragraph or two in this chapter because building a good fire is a skill many people have neglected to learn. When your fireplace is ablaze, it becomes the most compelling object in the room. Learning to lay the fire correctly is an easy and pleasant assignment.

The object is to have a fire that bursts readily into flame, burns brightly and evenly, and gives out heat while the smoke and fumes go up the chimney. Such fires, like anything well planned, don't simply happen. You will need three logs of approximately the same size, at least one of them split for faster combustion.

Although there are many ways to build a fire, this is probably the favorite: Open your damper wide. Then have at the ready those three logs, some split wood kindling of mixed hard and soft wood (pine is the obvious choice for the latter) and some newspaper. Crumple up the newspaper and use it as the bed of your fire. If you have a fire basket on legs, stuff the newspaper under it. Then lay two of the logs between the andirons, side by side, leaving a little space between them. If one is a bit green, use it as the back log, where it will be the last to ignite and the last to crumble.

Lay the kindling between the two logs like little bridges about an inch apart. The third log will be placed over this cradle of kindling. You have now built the foundation of a two-story fire, allowing ample space for the oxygen that good combustion requires. Light the newspaper at the botton of the fire. The pine kindling will burst into flame first, igniting the hardwood kindling, which in turn will send flames into the logs, seeking out gaseous pockets between the fibers until the three logs are also ignited.

Tend your fire neatly with poker, tongs, and brush. Replenish the mugs of cider, and ruminate. . . .

**Open-Fire Cooking**

While you're getting so proficient at fire making, you might as well do a little cooking, too. It gives you another chance to comb stores and yard sales looking for the perfect iron pot, the cooking chains or trammels and cranes, the ironware cooking vessels, spiders, corn poppers, hefty Dutch ovens, and antique outdoor cooking utensils. Cooking over an open flame, with or without a grill, requires a whole new kind of cooking utensil.

There's no reason why charcoal grilling should be limited to the outdoor season—as long as there is proper ventilation to carry off the carbon monoxide fumes that charcoal gives off when it burns. Some cooks like to mix charcoal and wood. Charcoal gives off almost twice the heat of wood, but wood ignites the slow-to-kindle coals.

Make sure that you can prepare food comfortably at your fireside. Provide for nearby table or counter space in your early planning. That way your indoor cooking can range from the simple but classic potato baked in the coals to a steaming *pot-au-feu* on a trammel. Add a grill, and you can start experimenting with a great variety of foods beyond the typical meat, onion, pepper and tomato combination that's even more delicious when it's been cooked over an open fire.

Although you might not want to prepare an entire dinner in a living room fireplace (you run the risk of filling the room with cooking odors and spattering fat), you will probably find no end of enjoyment in cooking food at your kitchen/dining hearth.

> "At last the great logs, crumbling low,
> Sent out a dull and duller glow."
>
> *John Greenleaf Whittier*
> Snowbound

The open fire is one of humanity's great comforts. A country home, even one with thermostat set unconscionably high, is never quite warm without one.

A Queen Anne wing chair and a cherry candle stand occupy the warming spot beside the fire in this living room. Hanging on the wall to the right of the mantel is an extremely rare pipe box.

The decorative cast iron stove was popular for a long time. Its great advantage was that it could be placed in a variety of locations, as long as its pipe would reach to an outside wall. This cast iron stove sits in a country schoolhouse.

The masonry fireplace served many purposes. People relaxed around the fireplace; they baked their food in it; and they slept nearby to take advantage of its warmth.

When the frost is on the pumpkin (out-of-doors), you can be sure it's time for Americans to cozy up to the fire indoors.

*The painted mantel lends formality to the country house, yet it is at home with simple authentic furnishings too. An Oriental rug adds to the charm.*

A Seth Thomas grand-father clock is placed to the right of the fireplace. A copper bedwarming pan hangs from the mantel. The shelf holds a salt-glaze decorated pitcher from the Shenandoah Valley, along with a tin candlestick.

Thoreau wrote: "Every man looks at his wood-pile with a kind of affection. I loved to have mine before my window."

# Country Windows

"Lights out. Shades up.
A look at the weather."
*Wallace Stevens*
*"Girl in a Nightgown"*

The shade on a city window keeps out prying eyes. The country window may have a shade too, but it's there to pull up so one can look out at the weather. Not just the weather, of course, but the morning snow on bare branches, the first feathery leaves of spring, or the mists rising from the valley. Since a country window is to look out of, its covering should be just enough to keep out the stark black of night or an overabundant amount of sun.

Traditionally, the country window was many-paned because glassmakers could not produce large panes. But eventually windows did get bigger and bigger, of course, until there was the picture window, then the wall-to-wall window. Now people are beginning to revive a fondness for the small, many-paned window. Much admired are the old-fashioned diamond-shaped leaded windows. If you have small-paned windows in your country house, cherish them. If you don't, you can buy a simulation in snap-in-place window frames

*If your windows need a bit of color, try short red curtains with a simple soft valance. And above the window, why not install a box shelf?*

that are easily removed for cleaning.

Another valuable old window is one of stained glass. Our forebears were enamored of these pieces of colored leaded glass through which sunlight poured into a room. Today, the craft is being revived all over the country, so you'll have no trouble finding new stained glass. Such a window is especially beautiful on an east or a west wall, where it catches the sun for longer periods of time, or in a bathroom where you may want privacy but not fussy window trimmings. Once you've installed a stained glass piece, you will understand why our ancestors were so fond of it.

### Window Coverings

Before you consider fabric at the window, think of shutters, a country natural. Shutters used to be an outside feature, but now they've moved indoors, where they can regulate light all day. Painted, stained, or varnished in their natural state, shutters can be used on nearly any window in the house. If your floors are a deeply stained walnut and your walls a light cream, try painting louvered shutters at the window a bright tomato red and carry the hot color into the room with another fabric.

Heavy exterior shutters can be used indoors for a rustic look: trellis-patterned shutters are a good choice for the kitchen or bath. A truly rustic shutter is a single panel of pine on a hinge. Shutters can also mask air conditioning units and appliances. Keep an eye out for old shutters someone might have foolishly thrown out. With any luck and a little retro-fitting, you might be able to use them, perhaps in combination with café curtains. Shutters are also a good answer for dormers; and if you carry them to the floor, they will make the windows look longer. Tall shutters that reach the floor can be used in other rooms as well.

Latticework is another way to avoid a fabric window treatment. If your window looks out on a garden, why not give it an arbor look? Make two swing-out frames of stock wood (see instructions at the end of this chapter) and install a shade behind them.

Decorative shades are yet another way to dispense with curtains. Matchstick or bamboo, wood venetian blinds, and fabric are all good choices for a natural look, especially for those windows too small to treat with anything elaborate. You also might want to pick up, for a shade, a stencil design used elsewhere in the room.

One more consideration before you decide to go with curtains: plants. You can create a healthy showcase for your plants by installing shelving right across the window. If there is also shelving on either side of the window, extend it right over the window and fill the shelves with African violets or a collection of cranberry glass or Bristol blue bottles. Like stained glass, they will catch the sunlight and filter prisms of light into the room.

Don't crowd those shelves with plants, however. Give each one a little space in which to be appreciated. Plants can be hung on a window too, either from rods installed across it or on brackets that swing out when you want to check the weather.

### Windows All Through the House

The living or family room windows in a country home can be hung with simplicity itself: full-length coarsely woven cotton that complements the wall. Or you can combine the homespun fabric with sheers that filter light so

*Antique bottles are a collector's item that can be displayed on a sill in front of the kitchen window. Light filters beautifully through the clear and tinted glass.*

successfully they don't cancel out a view.

If you're going to treat your windows to fabric, don't be skimpy. Better to buy less expensive draperies than to buy too little fabric. By using yards and yards of an inexpensive fabric like dime-store gingham, you can create a window that will really enhance a family room, instead of looking as pathetic as a young man in highwater trousers.

If the window wall is a focal point of your living room, try turning it into a unit by installing three bookshelves between the two windows and the wall as well. Then connect them overhead with a one-by-twelve-inch pine plank valance. Stain the wood dark mahogany and outfit the windows in openweave casement, macramé, interesting antique lace, or crochet work.

Another unifying use of wood is for those people who have found a store of old beams—enough, perhaps, to construct a barn-rafter look at your windows. Run one beam along the top of the windows, one at each wall, and the third in the middle. Then install Y-shaped support beams on the middle vertical beam and half a Y on each wall side. The support beams will form four isosceles triangles. Behind the beams you can hang your fabric, floor to top of beam, of pleated white duck, sheers or homespun. The fabric should be as plain and simple as possible.

Many a country living room has a bay window. Open it up by installing the valance and drapery across the front of the bay, not along the contour. For a Victorian parlor, you might want to consider a rich floral print tieback drapery and valance with crocheted, lace, or sheer undercurtains.

In a family room with built-ins under the windows for storage, create a little sitting nook with matching cushions and café curtains. Line a simple cotton solid or print and hang on a brass pole with brass rings. Add a few pillows and a bit of special needlework and you have an inviting window-seat. A small window may be ideal for a patchwork treatment; use one of those worn quilts you couldn't resist buying.

For a formal Victorian living room, you may want to drape a window with swags and tiebacks, jabots and fringe. The fabric should be of a good weight but should not be opulent. Velvet? Probably not, but how about a velvet ribbon trim?

Living room draperies, like everything country, should either be simple and unpretentious or gloriously old-fashioned. Thick wood dowels, stained dark and varnished to a high gloss, are more pleasing than the standard drapery hardware. Fabric loops can be slipped though the dowel, and the curtain can be easily swept aside to capture a view. Avoid the "prepared" look of the typical side-panel-at-each-end approach by hanging a single drapery that closes out the night or the too-bright sun.

Bedroom windows should be dressed in keeping with the rest of the room. If the look is simplicity itself, with a four-poster, a gaily colored quilt, a rag rug and a pine chest, consider an equally simple window treatment. If your bed must be placed on the window wall, consider hanging shirred homespun or chintz behind a window framed with pieces of ordinary two-by-four stock lumber in three panels. Or, if the window is not flanked by a bed, think about installing a shelf above an air conditioning unit. Facing it with lattice will make it turn into another inviting windowseat. Curtains should be hung to shelf height.

Your bedroom may cry out for traditional crisscross organdy curtains with fluted and ruffled borders, particularly if the fabric is carried onto a bed canopy or dust ruffle. Or you can use full-length chintz panels tied back with big bows.

On the other hand, your tastes might be ill suited to bows, and the view out your bedroom window may be just of the road. For those rare instances when the window is not a focal point of the room, consider a panel of folding screens. You can buy unfinished louvers and paint or stain and varnish them. Or you can buy panels with openings that can be fitted with fabric. This is a perfect use for that small amount of special crewel or embroidered linen you bought because you couldn't resist it. Keep your eye out for old-fashioned screens too. They can provide much interest in a simply furnished bedroom.

If your bedroom window has a great view, don't go overboard with valances, swags and jabots. Use light fabrics and a light touch. The country window is not something to cover up, but something to enhance as a frame for the great outdoors. Why compete? Just don't go overboard to make everything match.

Another idea: create a desirable niche in your country bedroom with draperies. Install a frame around a bed or couch sitting bed, without headboard, that extends along a full window wall. The standard twin-sized bed is thirty-nine inches wide. Allow an extra three inches for easy fitting. Remember, fabrics should be loosely hung. Enclose the bed with a niche frame of finished pine or walnut and hang tieback draperies on two sides of the bed. A shade that coordinates the wallpaper design, or a simple shutter, will look better than more fabric at the window. Within your little nook, throw some colorful pillows and hang a sconce lamp or two for reading. This draperied bed is a re-creation of the traditional bed favored by previous generations in rooms that were unheated during the night. If you can afford crewel or needlework draperies, you will be following an old tradition that still creates a sensational look. Or make it a winter project, embroidering your own bed-curtains in a personal style, or copying the tree-of-life design that was so popular in early American life. If the height of your window allows it, elevate the bed a little. Old beds were built high to avoid drafts. This cozy curtained niche will become a favorite retreat.

The kitchen/dining window treatment should be sweet and simple, allowing the light and the view to shine. One of the most important windows in your house is the one above the sink. Decorate it from both sides so your eye can light on something pleasing while you do your kitchen work. How about an outside windowbox filled with flowers in the summer and turned into a bird feeder in the winter? Or hang a lobelia plant to sway in the breeze, and limit your window curtain to a cheerful café with shutters, a crisp matchstick blind, or a colorful fabric shade.

Kitchen curtains make for decorating ideas that can sometimes really go wrong. The country house is not the place for cutesy kitchen window trimmings. Consider choosing your fabric outside the drapery department and making the curtains yourself. They are simple to sew, and much more satisfying than the typically uninspired store-bought kind.

Try hanging kitchen or dining room café curtains on wood rods with matching wood rings. A lumber yard will have them ready to finish. You can paint, or perhaps stain and varnish, to suit your color scheme. Café curtains are successful in the country because they can be whisked aside so easily. You don't want to burden a country house with complicated drapery hardware to push, pull and tug.

The fabric for these curtains can be a classic check, a calico, homespun, stripe or gingham—the simpler the better. Frames can also be built around dining room windows, allowing for a sheer undercurtain. Crisscross curtains look good with lots of wood and gleaming china, as do draperies trimmed in a color that matches the upholstery of the dining chairs.

Planning a corner-window eating nook gives you a chance to coordinate an entire area. Install a wood valance and hang a simple white duck Roman shade.

*America's collectibles appear everywhere. Victorian dolls decorated Rosalynn Carter's Christmas tree in the White House in 1981. During her husband's administration, Mrs. Carter brought to America's first house the best of American crafts. Rosalynn was a gracious and very knowledgeable First Lady, and I shall always admire her for the charm she brought to our country.*

Geraniums can be potted and brought indoors in the winter. How handsome these are against a light-filled window, with the snow for contrast in the background.

A country house is not complete without a fireplace, its true source of pleasure. An English oak table is the focal point of this room—set off by the fireplace, of course.

People tend to run out of ideas when they get to the bathroom windows. Often these are too small to do anything inspiring with, or they were placed in the room by the architect almost as an afterthought. Such bathroom windows usually need all the help they can get. Here are some suggestions:

Paint shutters to match the enameled bathroom wall. Or use laminated shades, matchstick blinds, ruffled sheers, or homespun with a row of cheerful fringe. Try setting moisture-loving plants on glass or lucite shelves. If you don't have to treat your bathroom window for reasons of privacy, why not sheet-mirror the wall opposite it to reflect some outside greenery?

For a child's bath, create your own geometric window screen by cutting out shapes your children have made. Apply to a shade with double-faced tape and then paint the remainder of the shade a bright color, remove the shapes, and you have a child's version of folk art hanging at the window.

Every house has a problem window or two. Dormer windows, slanting windows (particularly in A-frame ski houses), tiny windows too high to see out of, windows bulging with air conditioning units, or windows framed with a sunburst arch are not only decorating problems but also decorating possibilities. Leave a sunburst exposed in all its glory; or, if you want a drapery, have it installed at the highest point of the straight part of the frame; or frame your sunburst with a valance that matches its curve.

Frame a bay window, particularly if it exposes a view, with a scalloped valance or latticework. Use tiebacks for a more formal look, or keep the lattice treatment light and airy by hanging simple fabric shades. If your bay window doesn't go to the floor, treat it as if it did. The to-the-floor look is so much more attractive. Use one curved traverse rod for sheers and a straight-across-the-bay scalloped valance to pull it all together.

You can hang the dormer window with a shutter enameled in a bright scarlet, teal blue, or goldenrod—with a windowseat in a contrasting print. Or you can install a double tier of café curtains hung on poles for better control of light.

What to do with a skylight? An unshaded skylight can let in too much light for comfort at certain times of the day, and the best answer is a "constant tension" shade that works on cords that hold it firmly in place. But if sunshine is not a problem, frame the windows with wood beams and install a bottom-up shade for privacy.

If you're lucky enough to have a sliding glass window that looks out on a spectacular desert or mountain valley, let it be. People who live in glass

*The walls in this dining room are painted harvest yellow. A stencilwork border of grapes and vines crowns the room. The table is a double trestle, and the chairs are of the Hudson Valley Queen Anne style.*

*Country windows are often fitted with a single curtain.*

houses shouldn't shut out the view. Let nature do the decorating, and treat the window itself as a frame for the ever changing show outside. Use discreet shades for those times when you do want to shut out the light or the dark.

**How to Make Your Own Window Treatments**
Try a pinch-pleated drapery at home:
1. Measure the drapery rod and double that figure to determine what width the draperies should be.
2. Figure out the number of panels you'll need by dividing the width figure by the width of your fabric, minus two 2-inch seam allowances. Say, for example, your window is 99 inches wide. You'll need 198 inches of fabric. If

the fabric you're using is 36 inches wide, divide 198 by 32. You'll need six 32-inch panels. To find out how much material to buy, multiply the number of panels by the length measurement. Divide the resulting figure by 36 to convert to yards.

3. Cut out fabric on a flat surface, cutting just one panel first and using that panel as a pattern for the others. Cut the lining material 3½ inches shorter and 6 inches narrower than the drapery panel.

4. Hem draperies and lining separately. On draperies, make a 3-inch hem, double it over, and then hem again. Total depth should be 6 inches.

5. Place lining and drapery fabrics right sides together, raw top edges flush. Center lining so there's a 1¼-inch hem on either side, and stitch lining to drapery fabric. Turn right side out, and blindstitch drapery fabric hangover to lining.

6. Place commercial pleater tape and draperies right sides together. Stitch across top. Turn right side out, press, and stitch down along tape sides and bottom, under hook pockets.

7. Insert pleating hooks to make pleats. (The kind with locking devices are best for heavy fabrics such as duck.)

**How to Make a Paneled Screen**

A paneled screen can be anything from an open-out scrim, set inside a window, to a floor-to-ceiling, fold-up showpiece. You can make two types of paneled screen: a solid panel or a frame.

*A Solid Panel*

1. Buy cut-to-measure plywood to the height and width of the space you want to screen.

2. Glue or staple fabric or paper to the front and the edges of each panel. If you staple, staple only at edges, tucking corners as you do when wrapping a gift package. Spot gluing will help here. Trim excess fabric.

3. Seam a length of fabric, or cut a panel of paper to fit the back of the panel. Staple or glue the fabric or paper to the panel. If you staple, attach staples as close to edges as possible.

4. Trim edges with wood stripping, braid, gimp, or any border decoration.

5. Attach hinges by using screws, not nails. Border decoration can be cut away at hinges for easy attachment. The hardware store will tell you precisely what hinges to buy. (Be sure to bring with you the exact width of your panel edge.)

### A Frame Panel

1. Buy stock lumber boards: two-by-fours for a heavy, floor-to-ceiling panel; one-by-twos for a panel you will attach to a wall or window. Buy thin finishing strips the width of the boards; they will cover nails, hinges, and staples on the back of the frame.

2. Make your frame panels to fit width and height of the space you want to cover. First cut the boards to measure, then screw corners together with a straight or L-shaped metal plate. (The screws should come with the plate.)

3. With staples or glue, attach fabric or paper to the back of the screen.

4. Finish with wood stripping of the same width—but not the same thickness—as the boards, using finishing nails.

5. Paint the frame and the finishing strips either before or after the fabric or paper has been stapled to the back of the frame. It's easier if you paint before.

6. With hinges, attach the one-frame screen to the inside of your window. If your screen is multipaneled, first hinge panels together, and then attach screen to the window or let it stand free. (See instructions for solid panel hingeing, above.)

### How to Frame a Window in Wood or in Fabric-Covered Wood

1. Use one-by-ten-inch pine cut to fit. Miter the corners, using a miter board, or allow corners to meet flush.

2. Using a straight or an L-shaped hinge, screw corners together at the back of the frame.

3. Using the same L-shaped hinge, attach one-by-ten-inch side panels to the front frame. Finish with a piece of one-by-ten-inch board across the top of your frame (it's not necessary to finish the bottom).

4. Cover your frame in fabric if you like. Simply staple the fabric to the frame as you're building it. Hinges can be attached right through the fabric. See instructions on covering a paneled screen with fabric or paper.

### How to Stencil a Window Shade

With a design of your own:

1. Cut out the design you want to apply to the shade, using brown paper.

2. Apply it to your shade; using a nonpermanent adhesive—masking tape that has been folded so that it will stick to both design and shade makes a good nonpermanent adhesive.

3. Paint the whole shade any color you choose.

4. When the paint has dried, remove the brown paper. Your designs will

pop out in white.

With a wallpaper design:
1. Trace your wallpaper design on tracing paper with a stiff, heavy pencil.
2. Put the traced design on a sheet of heavy cardboard.
3. Press through the tracing paper as you redraw the design so that an impression is transferred to the cardboard.
4. With a matte knife (or razor) cut through the cardboard along the impressions.
5. Secure cardboard to the shade.
6. Using a stiff stencil brush and textile paint, work from edge to center until the stencil is filled in. Don't remove the stencil until the paint is dry. If you wish to use the same stencil in several different places on your shade, clean both stencil and brush before reusing. Again, don't remove the stencil until the paint is dry.
7. After twenty-four hours, apply an iron, set on low temperature, to the shade, using a pressing cloth over the shade for protection. If you want to stencil more than one color, a separate stencil must be prepared for each. And remember, all you stencilers, that white, room-darkening shades offer the best painting surface.

### How to Apply Fabric to Shades

First of all, don't try to sew fabric to a window shade. It will ripple or bunch.

For cutout fabric:
1. Cut out fabric designs.
2. Glue them to shade.
3. Allow glue to dry.
4. Paint edges of cutout fabric with colorless nail polish to prevent raveling.

For solid fabric:
1. Trim fabric to the exact width and rolled-out depth of shade, leaving a ¼-inch seam allowance.
2. Press seam allowances under, measuring carefully.
3. Carefully glue seams to back of fabric.
4. Allow to dry.
5. Working carefully and spreading the glue evenly, attach entire piece of fabric to shade.
6. Allow to dry.

Window frames and mullions on a country window can be painted—or they can be left natural. Note the contrast in these two Down Home rooms. One has a pine cupboard with a pine window casing; the other shows a white corner cupboard with a white-painted window casing.

Mullion windows are a popular choice of the Down Homer. Here a French-style window opens into a charming breakfast niche.

Every window should frame an appealing view. This wooden bench sits under a fir tree outside our country kitchen window. Pots of daisies decorate the arms of the bench.

*Windows outfitted with flower boxes always have great appeal. This one is filled with geraniums and vines.*

*The simpler the window treatment, the better. Here white cotton fabric has been hung from metal poles inside the window frame.*

*If you like conventional window treatments, choose a small Americana print for your draw curtains. These are hung at sill length.*

*Some country windows require no window treatment; if the view is a great one, why cover it up? On the other hand, I personally do not like to look at a sheet of black window at night, so I cover the pane with a film of white sheer.*

# Walls and Wallpaper

Think of your country house as a unit, with its walls—like the earth—a background for the display of your treasures. Treating all the walls alike by painting your entire house one pleasing color eliminates the problem of going from a rust room to a green one to a pink one and what to do with the doors that tend not to stay closed.

"How happy is the little stone
that rambles in the road alone . . .
Whose coat of elemental brown
a passing universe put on."

Emily Dickinson's coat of elemental brown may surprise you by its versatility and richness. If brown is too somber a color for you, how about rich

*Think nature's colors when selecting what is just right for the walls in the dining room. In our country house they are painted Indian clay. Wood beams have been stripped of their layers of old paint. The ceiling surfaces between the beams are painted Indian clay also.*

cream, or daffodil, or young lettuce, or flaming sumac? Choose your colors with a regard to the amount of available light as you move from room to room; and when you are in the paint store, remember that light colors dry darker on a wall and dark colors dry lighter.

When it comes to paint and pigment, the modern country dweller has the advantage, for once, of quality and ease of application over the country decorators of the past. Not only does the paint go on more easily with a roller, that great boon to wall color; but certain kinds of paint, particularly oil based, will also take a good scrub. Be sure to choose a washable paint for hallways or other areas where surfaces are likely to become smudged.

Today's country decorator can apply interesting textures to a wall with stucco paint, which is especially good for a rugged surface that needs a little masking. And best of all are those glorious custom-mixed colors! You may have gone through a meticulously restored historical room and admired a particular shade of slate blue, deep vermilion, or elemental brown, wishing you could duplicate it on your own country walls. Well, you can. Most good paint stores will provide you with color charts from which you can select clear, strong, traditional country colors, the ones nature herself puts on. Just remember: when buying special custom-mixed paints, be sure to buy enough plus a little extra for touch-up jobs. A second batch will rarely match the first, even if you have kept a record of the number. Avoid having to do another paint job by buying enough paint the first time. Take careful dimensions with you so the paint store clerk can help you figure out how much you need.

As to which color is the right backdrop for your country house, you may want to rekindle your imagination by reading the color section in "Country Style." What you want is a pleasing, unifying neutral color that will do justice to every room and area way. Is there a long, dark hall in your life? Do you have small rooms with small windows? Then choosing a rich bark shade or a steely slate blue or a deep plum may not work. But sky blue, goldenrod or warm melon may be just the thing. Walk through your rooms as you contemplate which of nature's elemental colors you can best visualize on your walls. Choose a clear, sunlit color, and stay away from murky, harsh colors that have the look of the chemistry set about them. They rarely look right anywhere, these standard institutional greens, yellows, pinks and blues that look like nothing nature ever made, but in a country house they will be especially dreary.

Painting the entire house one color will result in a kind of serenity as people move from room to room, remarking, "There's something so restful about your house." That's because the background doesn't keep changing. However, few will even realize that every room in your house has been treated alike! It's not the walls that you want to command attention but what you put on them, and you are in for some pleasant surprises when you see how effective books, paintings, a pile of colorful pillows, or old-fashioned lace curtains will look against a background of rich eggplant, country cream or pale raspberry.

How about woodwork? If it's never been painted, don't you be the culprit. If it has been, give it a coat of oil-based gloss enamel for easy cleaning. Some people like the look of gloss on flat wall surfaces as well. If you are doing your own paint job, remember that enamel is a finishing coat, and applying more than one coat results in unsightly blisters and cracks. Use several coats of prime on a problem wall before you brush on the final color coat. Although oil-based paint is more expensive, you'll be glad in the long run that you chose it for your woodwork because of its scrubbability.

### Small, Dark Areas

An almost universal feature of the country house is the small room. People built such houses for maximum warmth and economy; they rarely had the luxury of considering the vista outside or the quantity of light that came through those typically small windows. Since expanding a small, dark room with a wall of mirrors may be inappropriate in a country room, consider a

*Small-flower wallpapers are the perfect answer for the walls in the upstairs bedroom, where one of the many available patterns can be used handsomely.*

background color throughout of white tempered with a pigment to reduce the harshness. A bit of clear red will produce a strawberries-and-cream look, and cream can also be used on the ceilings and woodwork. Strong green mixed with white will yield a pale lettuce shade, or a bit of purple and umber will produce a subdued mauve. All these shades will lighten a room without your having to resort to stark white.

### Wide Open Spaces

On the other hand, your home may have some open areas you would like to make more intimate. Here's where you can indulge yourself in strong, glorious, natural colors, inspired by the view from the window. Blackberry, mustard, zinnia red, or pine green: take a look around, and remember those pleasing deep shades when you're pondering the paint store's color charts.

### Other Country Wall Problems

Do you have a damaged wall with cracks or unsightly patches of plaster? Consider using one of the thick texture paints on such a wall. The look of plaster is truly authentic, and once you have applied the texture paint (think twice before using taco-shop stucco: overuse has made that look a cliché), you can apply color. There's no rule that says a plaster wall has to be whitewash white.

Another common decorating problem in the country house is a low ceiling. Stay away from dark colors, which lower the roof and will only add to the Alice-in-Wonderland claustrophobia. A light color can raise the roof; but light doesn't necessarily mean white.

Do you have a long, narrow hallway? Usually there's one that connects the upstairs bedrooms, adding another headache—all those doors. Try this approach to widen the look: install a dado or wainscotting. Typically it is 32 inches high, including the baseboard. Wainscotting can be bought by the foot at a lumber yard, or you can keep an eye out for used wainscotting at demolition sites. You may not be able to buy exactly what fits your dimensions, but if you're lucky you will, and the old is always more interesting than the new. If you'd like to try a dado in your upstairs hall, first take some measurements. With a folding rule, measure your wall up from the floor and draw a line at 29 inches. This is the line along which the bottom of the chair-rail molding will be nailed to the wall. This molding is typically 3 inches, and the width of the dado will be 32 inches minus the width of the baseboard. Ideally, the baseboard should be the same width as the chair rail, but if it's not, don't fret. You certainly don't want to start ripping out the original baseboard.

While you're at the lumber yard, you might also want to take a look at molding, which comes in many interesting widths and styles. Choose from quarter- and half-round, astragal, and pressed molding; and widths from ¼ to 2 inches. A survey of the kinds of molding you can buy may inspire you to finish off your country walls and doors with a frame of molding. It can be painted either the same color as the walls or a contrasting color.

Back in your hall, consider painting the walls above your wainscotting a bright, cheerful lemon, or melon, or sky blue, or whatever backdrop color you've chosen. A wallpaper with a stenciled look or a neat stripe can also be good-looking. Paint all those doors, as well as the louvered shutters you may want to install on the end wall window, in a semigloss. If you want to widen your hall, install a rag carpet with an interesting, perhaps irregular, horizontal stripe.

Doors, doors everywhere. You will want to paint them the same color as the walls to make them disappear into the backdrop if they are placed at irregular points of the room—that is, in ways that break up the symmetry. On the other hand, if the doors are well balanced—if an entry door balances a closet door, for instance—then you can paint all the doors, dado and woodwork in a contrasting color.

Ready with the paint, the moldings, the dado, the rollers, brushes and drop cloths: on goes the coat of elemental color, the hues of the earth or sky, a field of grain or a delicate wildflower, dusky gray or weathered nut brown, the clear and lively young shades of spring or the rich, ripe hues of autumn or the somber, restful colors of winter to frame your cheerful treasures. Whatever your choice, you will have given your house one pleasing, unifying color as a background for bright additions: patchwork pieces, portraits and landscapes, shelves full of books and treasures, your meticulously restored wood pieces, the carefully chosen fabrics at windows and on upholstered pieces, and even that intriguing farm implement that looks as if it had been designed by a country Calder.

## Wallpapers

In the early days of our country, only the wealthy could afford to paste expensive sheets of paper on their walls. The paper was costly, and it came in tiny sheets not much bigger than writing paper. More humble folk, ever adept at emulating the rich with what they could afford, drew wallpaper designs directly on the wall. In today's country home, the stenciled wall is valued more highly than fancy wallpaper, and the fancy designs of another era do not please so much as wallpaper patterns that imitate the simple, tidy look of the stencil.

Stencils were often applied by itinerant jack-of-all-artists who would also paint a portrait or even a wall. Stencils were used to cover a whole wall to look like wallpaper or used as a border around doors and ceilings. Patterns were adaptations of popular wallpaper designs, simplified because of the limitations of the cut-and-daub method. The stencil reduces a design to its elemental simplicity, which is why it works so well in a country home. You can buy stencil kits and apply popular patterns of the past, or you can make your own stencils: trace a design on onionskin paper, then transfer it to a sheet of sturdy cardboard with carbon paper. As you do so, you will see why stencil designs are the essence of simplicity—a daisy with a single leaf, a cluster of grapes joined by tendrils, star-and-geometric hexlike patterns. The process reduces a design to a few bold, tidy lines. You can even get a little fancy and use two or three sets of stencils for a multicolored design.

Combining stencils and a painted wall is one way to finish off a room. Another is to use wallpaper that has the handblocked look of a stencil. Remember the old-fashioned hatbox covered in floral-and-stripe paper? That kind of small design works well. If you choose a simple flower and leaf motif, try using it above the dado in that dark hall. Paint the dado a sprightly goldenrod, and paper both wall and ceiling.

Another favorite wallpaper in a country home is the stripe, which also helps raise the typically low country ceiling. Vertical ticking, irregular widths, and floral stripes all work well. If you are papering a bedroom, paper the closet too. But stay away from multicolored stripes in a closet, as clothes tend to get lost against that confusing background. Horizontal stripes can also make a small room appear larger.

Textured wallpapers are appropriate in a country home; grasses, burlap, and other nubby materials are ideal. Fancy flocked wallpaper, however, is not. Printed fabric can also supply the look you want. You may have more success if you are looking at fabric than you will have with wallpaper, particularly those fabric collections that are replicas of popular designs. If your walls are very smooth, you might consider using those wonderful imported wrapping-paper designs. They're larger, at least, than the old Colonial import papers, and with a little patience will go up wrinkle-free. Then you can apply several coats of varnish. There are many pleasing wrapping-paper

Good old off-white paint can easily be applied by the do-it-yourselfer. In this country bathroom with a Victorian touch, the walls are neutral off-white. Pictures are hung from wire attached to the crown moulding for the real Down Home look.

prints—colorful paisleys or neat stripes and checks, or small repetitious country scenes that may require a little patient matching. However, this thin paper can only be applied to a wall that is in good condition.

To determine how many rolls of wallpaper you will need, measure the perimeter of the room. Add to the sum of the four walls the distance from floor to ceiling, but not including the baseboard. Multiply the height by the perimeter, and divide by 30. Although there are 36 square feet in a roll of wallpaper, allowance must be made for matching and mistakes. The amount you need is then further reduced by allowing for windows and doors. Multiply width by height and divide by 30 for each, and then deduct from the total.

Wallpapering requires time and patience. Don't try to do a big job in a short time. When you do your selecting, get complete instructions about what is best for the kind of paper you are hanging, whether it is prepasted or peel-and-stick, or requires a mix of wheat paste and water. The success of wallpaper in a country home is the combination of warm wood, cheerful paint, and a pleasing repetition of design on the wall.

### Wood Walls

Real wood is the only kind that really works in the country, and the wood that usually works best is pine. Oak is for English drawing rooms, but pine provides rustic warmth as few other woods do. The best source for wood paneling is the demolition site or junkyard. Wood too weathered to use on a floor or as a tabletop may be perfect, in all its rugged glory, for a wall. There is always the standard tongue-and-groove wood paneling, but unless you can afford real wood, put your money elsewhere. This paneling typically comes in four-by-eight-foot sheets, to be nailed or glued to studs attached to the wall at intervals of sixteen inches. Irregular walls call for an expert, but a fireplace wall may be simple enough for you to tackle yourself. If you've come across a beautiful piece of barn siding or similar old wood, it might be just enough for that important wall. Check local codes for the distance required between the wood wall and the opening of the fireplace.

Installing wood on a wall is also a good way to insulate a room, and it's less expensive than ripping out a wall and insulating between the inside and outside walls. If you have a drafty north room, think of wood. It will warm it twice, once with its substance and again with its style. Wood can also be stained and varnished to match floors, moldings or dados. It's almost impossible to use too much wood in a country home. It also looks great on the ceiling. Narrow-board tongue-and-groove wood ceilings were once common. If you are fortunate enough to have original ceiling paneling, restore it with love.

As to caring for your wood paneling, check "Refinishing Old Country Wood" in this book. Stick to the real thing if you can—then cherish it, care for it, and pass it on.

## Filling Up the Wall

Something there is that does not like a bare wall, especially in the country. In fact, the tendency is toward too much on the wall in a country home, so great are the temptations of country collecting. The best way to decorate is to start with fresh, clean walls, and begin putting things on them one at a time. Let surprises happen, and learn to capitalize on the unexpected.

A great space saver in a small country house is the wall cabinet. Old-fashioned country houses once boasted of many small hanging cupboards, some that fitted neatly into corners. Or you may prefer the tidy look of built-ins, which can be painted the same color as the wall and virtually made to disappear. You might want to coordinate antique wall cabinets with some sturdy shelving for books. An entire wall of simple pine shelving installed from floor to ceiling (no back is necessary) can be filled with books, music and art. The shelving can be designed with pegs so that shelves can be adjusted. A country home must have a place for books, and putting them all together in one place is another way of warming a room. Books that look as though they'd been bought by the yard (with matching tooled leather covers) are somehow not so genuinely warming as a wall of books in many sizes, well thumbed because they are well loved. Establish some order in your eclectic library by adjusting shelves to accommodate the varied sizes of your reading material. There are people who remove the dust jackets from books before they put them on the shelf. What's wrong with a little color? Books from floor to ceiling look wonderful in narrow areas between windows, or running along the wall below the windows with cushions above. These are country windowseats, and no house is really Down Home without them.

Is there any wall space left? Ah yes, over there. . . . Walls fill up fast. Make sure what you put there means something to you, and is not there just because it matches the colors in the draperies. People complain a lot about the trials of picture hanging. Mistakes leave gouges in walls, and getting them even is so tiresome, and can you hang pictures on a print wall, even one with a big, bold pattern? Yes, pictures can be hung on a printed wall, even one with a big, bold pattern, but set off the picture with a color contrasting with the paper in the frame plus a colorful mat for better appreciation of the picture. The mat can be the same color as one of those in the wallpaper. Hang large-scale pictures on a small-print wallpaper, and any size pictures on a large-scale design, provided they are well matted and framed in contrasting colors. Striped wallpapers make an especially good backdrop for pictures.

As you grow into your country home, the things you hang on the wall will come and go like the seasons, changing as you change. But the well-unified house-of-one-color will always keep it together, from room to room, as treasures come and go.

*A painted white stucco wall behind a wall-hung hutch makes a good neutral background for pewter and other collectibles.*

A charming small-field-flower wallpaper covers the walls in the children's room at Sagamore Hill. Doors and mouldings are all wood stained—as are the mouldings in all the other rooms in the house.

The dining room at Teddy Roosevelt's Sagamore Hill is strong and heavy in its style. The walls are covered with a simple green-on-white paper. The dark-stained beams and doors lend a somewhat masculine look to the setting.

The wagon seat set against a brick wall draws the eye here. Brick walls furnish the right background for country style, both inside and outside the house.

Try a log cabin wall in your country living room. The natural timber here gives a homespun background for a handsome original country cupboard.

In the corner of the dining room the stenciled border detail of grapes and vines is prominently seen. The cupboard has raised panel doors and its original hinges as well as original paint. Dating from 1720, it is from Deerfield, Massachusetts. Next to the cupboard is a three-slat ladder-back pilgrim chair which dates from about 1690.

Decorate walls with pictures, large and small—and with accessories too. Brackets to hold real candles are always the right look, as are antique cooking utensils.

# *Outdoor Decorating*

A lot of Down Home living is done outdoors. This chapter will cover exteriors and what to do with them, from lanterns to yard swings, shutters to fences, screen doors to tree houses. Just as important to a successful Down Home look is what *not* to do to achieve that indefinable quality that causes passersby to crane their necks looking backward, not because they've seen something opulent and grand, but for a second look at something familiar and inviting. You will want to feel that way when you catch your first glimpse of your own country home, too. Down Home, that first glimpse, is a leap in the heart that cannot be fully explained or even fully understood. It goes without saying that there are no pink flamingos, no showy Greek fountains or sophisticated urns on the lawn; no fancy Louisiana wrought iron grillwork or magenta shutters on a house painted stomach-medicine pink; no wooden Vikings in the driveway—nothing that takes one's eyes away from the overall landscape.

*Through the woods and over the bridge to Nicky and Sebastian's log cabin playhouse. There are flower boxes filled with petunias at the two front windows. The interior of the toy house is furnished with a stool and a play sink.*

The guidelines for the outside are much the same as they are for the inside: functional beauty, comfort, authenticity. Modesty is optional, if to violate it means Victorian gingerbread or a room full of folk art. Out-of-doors, however, there is one additional rule: Do not make choices that will contrast with mother nature. Blend instead.

Exteriors are always important, but never more so than in the country, where the wrong choice is like a billboard that shouts DISASTER! Avoid making mistakes by becoming a conservative in the true sense of the word—one who preserves and protects the best of the past. The best of our own past is the hand hewn, the natural object turned into a functional one, the sturdy and skillfully crafted piece that has withstood the test of time. Such are the raw materials of the Down Home look, especially out-of-doors: the stump, the bench, the swing, the hinged shutter. And lots of flowers . . .

### Flowers

A country house is not complete without flowers everywhere—growing up its sides and around its footings, and bursting from containers at every level.

But not just any flower will do. Learn the names of the old-fashioned varieties and plant them. This will involve you in the reading of seed catalogs in February and March—an important Down Home ritual. "So *that's* what a cockscomb looks like! Wouldn't it look nice against the north fence?"

Country yard favorites tend to fall into two types: the vivid splash and the heady fragrance. Foremost among the gaudy ones are zinnias, marigolds, and geraniums. The heavily scented include lilacs, peonies, roses, and lilies-of-the-valley. Aficionados know that the only way to enjoy them to their fullest is to cup them to your face—which you do almost instinctively—and drink deeply. Don't forget to make room for the ones that delight the children: hollyhocks for making dolls with graceful red or pink petal skirts; buttercups to tuck under the chin to determine whether one likes butter; snapdragons that open and close their mouths.

There are so many lovely varieties to choose from: feathery cosmos that grows thigh high; spikes of delphinium ranging from pale to midnight blue; foxglove and Canterbury bells; Shasta daisies and painted daisies and irises and fluttery coleus. Generally, rigid-stemmed flowers should be grouped with trailing ones. And keep an eye out for color: country flowers are not shy and retiring. Use the boldly colored ones as borders. Some are at their best when used alone, like frilly petunias or a sea of blue bachelor's buttons

*Our cat Pumpkin enjoys his morning chow under the wooden tavern bench that sits on our latticed back porch.*

*A pine cabinet fills a corner of the mud room of our 1795 house on Hillandale Farm. Accessories on the shelves include a collection of rabbits and other treasures belonging to the lady of the house, as well as clay vases for small flowers. Our cat, Christina—mother of Pumpkin, Root Beer and Snowy—guards the room.*

(maybe you think of them as cornflowers). Marigolds and tulips look best when planted in single colors. But zinnias bloom in shades that enhance one another; let them provide the great cornucopia of color that most people think of when they envision a country garden. Zinnias are the Breughels of a yard; they fairly vibrate with color. Use them in a generous bed for a massive display of yellow, orange, pink, red and white. They are also perfect for an immense bouquet.

See your yard as a palette. The seed packets can provide a color guide as you plan your plantings.

Geraniums, shunned for years because they were considered too common, are now back in favor, and fascinating new hybrids are being developed all the time. One recent variety, the Martha Washington, is a delicate rosy white that looks more like an orchid than a geranium. Common indeed! There are also tree geraniums and vining geraniums; and some varieties have rose- or lemon-scented leaves. Geraniums started from seed can produce startling and unusual shades of salmon, lemon or fuchsia. It is not at all difficult to renew your love for geraniums; and because they bloom so profusely and love the full sun, they are a perfect yard flower.

On the shady side of the Down Home house, you will usually find a bed of lilies-of-the-valley. Give them a start, and they'll return and spread every spring. Nosegays of these delicate white bells along a slender stem were once traditionally combined with violets for graduation bouquets, since they bloomed simultaneously in May. No yard is complete without these sweet-smelling shade-loving flowers.

Two other country favorites are lilacs and peonies, whose fragrance is one of the great joys of Down Home life. Both are native to the colder climates—which places them among the few advantages for the gardener of living in a northern zone. Lilac bushes make a fine high hedge, and a row of peonies a beautiful low one.

Another old-fashioned flowering shrub to grace the front of your house is spirea, a small-leafed bush that fairly explodes with starbursts of delicate white fronds every June, which made them a perennial ingredient of the wedding bouquet in a bygone era.

Country flowers also climb. If trellises and arbors have appeal for you, consider sweet peas, renowned for their fragrance, or clematis or floribunda roses.

Country flowers are by nature willing and prolific. Some will self-sow—whether you want them to or not—which is why they are called volunteers. One such ready-and-willing volunteer is the hollyhock. Unless you want it to take over your yard, confine it to a fence row or plant it along a barn wall.

To show off your plantings to their best advantage, grow them in containers positioned all around the house and yard, along the driveway, to define an outside eating area, or to mask the compost pile or a scrap heap. Containers can be tubs or boxes, groupings of clay pots, vessels of mortared stone or brick. Avoid "cute" containers whose color, shape or motif draws undue attention to themselves.

Whenever possible, allow any natural barrier to act as a line of demarkation between your lawn and your flower beds. Where none exists, a good solution is to lay down railroad ties, setting them partially into the earth.

A great spot for a splash of color is the intersection of your driveway and the public road. Welcome your guests with a whiff of country fragrance from a barrel filled to overflowing with pink petunias.

In Europe, especially in England, no matter how congested their living space, homemakers always seem to find room for a box or two of flowers. And when Manhattanites in our own country care enough to plant flowers in tubs set alongside the garbage cans and on sweltering high-rise rooftops, it seems almost sinful not to grow an abundance of them around a country house. Surround your dwelling with a floral offering to nature. Show her a generous display of color, wafts of intoxicating fragrance. You will be rewarded by the summer sound of bees buzzing, and hummingbirds and butterflies will make pilgrimages to your yard.

And you will always be ready to offer your departing guests a pair of clippers with which to cut an armload of fresh flowers to take with them back to the city.

## Outdoor Colors

Have you ever said to yourself as you drove by a country house: "How could anyone live with that ghastly color?" For a townhouse, a pink or aqua exterior is inoffensive enough, and in fact those colors look spectacular against white Mediterranean sands; but against a background of corn waving in the breeze, they look completely out of place. Avoid flamingo pink, magenta and buttercup yellow if your area is predominantly green. Instead, paint your farmhouse an off-white; and, to blend with the surrounding foliage, use one of the no-fail outdoor shades of deep green—hunter, forest, or Adirondack: more blue than yellow—on the shutters.

Another sure winner is brown. How can it offend? It's the color of the earth.

The rule for painting the house itself also applies to the furniture and accessories outdoors: Don't use colors that compete for attention with mother nature. Stick to green, white, brown and black; the neutral hues of stone and brick; and the natural tones of the various woods. When choosing outdoor colors, the most we can hope to achieve is a harmonious blend with nature. Remember, we're on her turf.

**Trash to Treasure**

Country things are getting expensive, but by encouraging your imagination and developing a sharp eye, you may find much of what you need for outdoor living in a dump pile, that great heap of country junk and treasure. You may be in for a surprise if you examine every article with the idea of turning it into something you can use in some way outside your house. And remember, indoors you may get away with a reproduction, but in the clear light of day all objects reveal their true selves. The real thing is mandatory for outside furnishings.

If your acreage was once a farm, have you looked up the real estate records? Who lived on your place before you? Finding out can be mysterious and exciting. The ownership of a piece of land goes far beyond the possession of a piece of paper. Once you begin examining its tangible past with a curious eye, you will learn to appreciate the permanence of a piece of the earth. Approach it as if it were a midden heap and you were an archeologist. Then, every spring plowing will become a dig where you may turn up such treasures as hand-hewn hinges with leather straps, a cast iron Model T toy car, old bottles, a scrolled boot scraper, a brass kettle with a lip, an arrowhead, some clam shells (curious . . . was this area once under water? or was it just that Indians once ate mussels and clams in this meadow?)

Even the rickety old farm buildings can be put to good use. The worn gray wood of an abandoned chicken house is highly prized by country decorators. The silvery surface of unpainted aged wood siding cannot be duplicated, and if an outbuilding is carefully dismantled, you can salvage the lumber for use as paneling or picture frames or something wonderful you haven't even thought of yet. If you want to leave it standing, the chicken house makes an ideal potting shed; a lean-to tool house can be converted to a writer's hideaway, a spring house to a wine cellar. Or transport an abandoned box car or school bus to your land and turn it into a play house.

*A pine table in the corner of our kitchen is used for break-
fast, lunch and sometimes Saturday dinner. All the chairs
are different. The wooden hayfork between the two windows
was purchased in a country barn.*

### Doors

If you're lucky, your country home still has its original front door of solid hardwood, with well-turned moldings and a beveled glass window. Those old doors not only look and feel solid and substantial; they sound sturdy: they close with such a satisfying thud. Few modern doors are built so sturdily. If your old door has long since been removed, be on the lookout for a replacement of a similar vintage. If you find one, it can be installed in a new jamb cut to size. Then hang an old bicycle basket on it and fill it with cut flowers that change with the seasons.

Another stroke of luck would be to find your original screen door still intact. What presto-chango aluminum wonder can compare with the old-fashioned wood-frame door with its cross wire, turned-wood spindles, and a certain creak on the long slow swing that was one of the unmistakable sounds of summer? With the old screen door, there is a certain satisfaction in the feeling of wood under the hand. Some people never quite get used to the coldness of metal and its clanking sound, particularly on the front door, and they rebel against the idea of the storm and screen combination for reasons of esthetics. All that cold metal between them and the view!

### Shutters

Sometimes, in the clear country air, starlight and moonlight are so bright they interfere with sleeping. This is when you will appreciate hinged shutters. Maybe you didn't realize that those attractive painted boards alongside the windows are designed to serve a useful purpose: They were meant to open and close! When they are hinged, they can be used throughout the day to admit or shut out the sunlight, and they can make a room comfortingly dark for an afternoon siesta. And at bedtime, nothing beats the snug feeling of battening down all the shutters and crawling under the covers for a long winter's sleep.

Ideally, shutters should be installed with fine old hand-forged hinges with black straps. These hinges are an example of old country hardware for which there is no modern counterpart. They help to explain why so many people gather at country demolition sites, where everything that comes down is of some use to someone. Recycling has never gone out of fashion in the country, where to buy something new is still a last resort.

### Porches

The porch was once a symbol of rural affluence: If fortune smiled, country people added a porch, then perhaps another. Soon porches were sprouting on houses all over the country, from front to rear and often from side to side. Sometimes balconies were added, or porticoes or widow's walks. Porches were screened in or glassed in to enhance their comfort and convenience. When good fortune smiled again, they were insulated so they could be used all year round.

In time, porches became passe, replaced across the land by picture windows and patios. Fortunately there are still plenty of them left Down Home, because country people do not feel bound to follow the fads. Tear off the porch? Where else can we sit and listen to the rain, relax comfortably as we watch the Fourth of July fireworks, or wave to friends passing by, or read or rock or woo or sleep on hot summer nights?

Indispensable though a porch is for a lot of country people, furnishing it can pose a problem. A front porch is a semi-private place, neither within nor outside of the house. It may require shading that can provide a measure of privacy without keeping out the breezes. A good choice is the roll-up blind made of wood, grasses, canvas, or coarsely woven cloth. Or you can install shutters or wooden venetian blinds. Whatever you choose, make it simple, subdued, and sturdy.

The classic porch furniture is of painted wood. Green, gray, white or brown porch enamel looks well with wood, especially wicker, as do those newly revived floral drapery prints that were all the rage after World War II.

A swing is a must for the Down Home porch. It can be suspended on chains from the ceiling, or it can glide back and forth within a frame. A wonderful choice is the wooden one with a slat-back that was once very popular in the Midwest and the South. Now it's hard to find, so take care of yours if you're lucky enough to have inherited one.

Decorate for function on the porch. It is not a place for personal accessories. Provide for what you need, and then make sure the furnishings are porchlike: A table or other surface to set a glass of lemonade or a plate of molasses cookies; a light to read by; some attractive pillows, a rag rug—nothing fancy. For the truly authentic touch, add a row of potted African violets.

The porch is one of the truly American institutions. You may soon wonder how you managed to live without one.

### Yard Furniture

Outdoor furniture must meet two important requirements: it must be

*This wooden cart is an auction find that I hope will be passed on from generation to generation. We sometimes fill the cart with apples or peaches—or, for a summer party, grapes.*

durable, and it must blend with the environment. Happily, within those limitations there is a wide selection of outdoor items for eating at, sitting on, or swinging in. Keep in mind that outdoor furniture must withstand suntan oil, sudden cloudbursts, searing heat, sprawling bodies, skate tips, and blowing dirt and sand. Obviously, the sturdier the better; and the best are pieces that look almost as if they were actually growing there in the yard.

Begin with nature's own resources. A tree stump properly sawn becomes a natural bench or table. Stones with interesting seatlike contours may be cushioned with patches of velvety moss.

Manufactured or converted benches are the best alternative to what nature has to offer. Spot them in convenient and unexpected places. Benches can be built around a tree or set into a wall. They can be made from old watering troughs or worn buggy seats; perhaps there are even some likely bench candidates in your pile of found objects.

The park bench, with its dark green wood slats and wrought iron sides, is one of those universal designs that can't be improved upon. It is actually much more comfortable than it appears. There are probably many near-perfect places for such benches in your yard. And of course they are absolutely essential for those people who feel a compulsion to sit down frequently to ponder nature. One country dweller has even brought a bench into his tomato patch for nocturnal meditation.

As for proper chairs, a great favorite is a heavy wooden slatted chair that sits low in the grass. These chairs can be made surprisingly comfortable with the addition of cushions, covered, of course, in a fabric that's water and greaseproof.

The classic deck chair has become a coveted item. The real thing is costly, but good reproductions can be bought reasonably. Canvas folding chairs are also comfortable and a good economical alternative. Be sure to choose an unobtrusive color.

*The sun coming through the trees casts charming and mysterious shadows on an old wicker rocker moved from the Down Home porch to the lawn.*

There must be a swing in the yard too, preferably a very high one: Is there anyone in the world who can resist a swing in a tall tree?

For those who prefer to do their swinging in a horizontal position, there is, of course, the hammock. A hammock suspended between two trees is what many people see when they close their eyes and dream of a vacation in the country. Some make lists of the books they will need to buy to read between catnaps; others plan just to lie there, undisturbed by the sound of the telephone, for hours and days on end.

As every hammock lover knows, comfort is not necessarily guaranteed. If real comfort is a must, the top of the line is the Pawleys Island hammock. This rope-and-wood combination is the economic mainstay of an island off the coast of South Carolina, where it is hand-crafted by the children. Other favorites for comfort are of wood and canvas, preferably of the awning type.

For those who like company in their hammocks, there's the Yucatan string hammock, which is free-form and can be hung from three or more trees.

Pleasant and comfortable facilities for eating are just as important outside the house as inside—perhaps more so. The blue ribbon usually goes to the sturdy X-based picnic table with attached seats. It is virtually indestructible and can safely be left outside the year round. Leave it unpainted, but keep it well scrubbed, and treat it now and then to an application of wood preservative. Such a picnic table soon begins to look like part of the scenery. Don't spoil the effect by putting up an umbrella. Like New Orleans grillwork or modern concrete statuary, umbrellas somehow just don't look at home Down Home.

The patio approach to which we are accustomed isn't the right one for outdoor cooking Down Home, where it should still look like the serious business it once was. A simple hibachi placed on a bed of bricks will sooner or later evolve into a fireplace of some kind for people who are serious cooks and eaters, because eating outdoors is one of the great joys of country living. Build your fireplace with natural materials rather than concrete. If you must use concrete, paint it dark green.

## Don't Forget the Children

Maybe you have children of your own, or maybe you want your grandchildren to come "over the river and through the wood" to visit you. Just as country kids are sometimes bewildered by the city, city children may need a little gentle guidance in the art of having fun in the country. But not much. Introducing them to a tree house is usually sufficient, after which you may see them only when they are hungry or tired. Let them participate in the building. Incorporate their ideas. Or maybe you can turn an old shed into a warming house.

If you have a creek or a pond, make them a raft. Or collect inner tubes. The bigger ones, once used on tractors, are ideal; but unfortunately they are hard to find.

An inner tube, a raft, a house built in the trees or nestled in the hedge: your children will be in heaven. Teach them to play safely. If you had the good fortune to spend your childhood or any part of it in the country, think back to the fun things you did, and recreate them for the new batch of kids. They will love you for it, and the plaintive sound of "There's nothing to do around here" will never be heard in your home.

### Lighting

When the sun goes down, the lights go out: That's the country.

In the city, the light provided for us at night by the municipality may be harsh and garish. The eerie mercury street lights that are installed to deter crime cast sinister shadows that create an atmosphere of high anxiety. We have no say in the way our city world is illuminated. In the country, we do.

It is essential to have a light burning somewhere near your house at night in case of an emergency. And you will want lights to welcome arriving guests, expected or not; or just to serve as a home beacon to the midnight stroller.

The quality of light must be right for the setting. In Amish country, a common sight is the twinkling of a pierced tin lantern beside the door. This simple four-sided fixture is easy to duplicate in wood: Cut four wood panels, bore holes in them, fit them into a box shape, attach the "box" to a bracket, insert a light bulb, and hang it beside your door.

However you decide to light your front door, make sure the fixture is worthy of its place. If you have come upon an antique carriage lantern, for example, that can be rewired, it should be scraped of its crustiness and polished to that worn but respectable patina of wood or metal that proclaims that it has been well weathered in the great outdoors. Check the "Country Collectibles" chapter for more about outdoor lanterns.

You may also want to light the most attractive areas of your yard so that you can admire the garden at night and at the same time extend the perimeter of your security. Keep the lighting soft and yellow. Lights can be positioned low in the shrubbery, or at the very top of the house or barn. A

*A Pawleys Island hammock hangs between two locust trees.*
*Here the children can swing or mommy and dad can rest*
*during the hot summer days and nights.*

247

light in a tall tree is a cheerful sight as it blinks on and off with the movement of the leaves in the breeze.

Approach your house slowly, or stand on the road at night, and decide where you want your night lights; but don't go overboard. Take care that your lighting will never disturb anyone's sleep.

### Fences

"Something there is that doesn't love a wall,
That sends the frozen-ground-swell under it . . . "

Robert Frost
*Mending Wall*

Nature does seem to rebel at being fenced in. Changes in temperature cause the earth to heave and crack; stone walls crumble and wood rots. But it's important to have the bounds of your property well marked.

Although fences can be made of brick, stone, or even foliage, the favorites seem to be of wood. The post-and-rail type is easy to build and to care for and makes a wonderful background for plantings. Usually constructed of a strong wood such as locust, it is cut to fit together like the familiar child's toy, without nails or glue. This fence makes a good backdrop for tall flowers like hollyhocks or sunflowers, or bright ones like marigolds.

Another classic wooden enclosure is the Tom Sawyer type of picket fence. Wide board or narrow, straight across the top or peaked, this fence is traditionally painted white. It too becomes an excellent background for flowers, at the same time providing privacy and protection from the wind.

In certain parts of the country, some type of fence is almost essential. On hilly terrain, stone fences are ideal. Open areas call for minimal fencing, with ranch posts widely spaced. Close-together high pickets make a perfect windbreak against ocean breezes. The right fence anywhere is the one that makes sense, the one that blends most naturally into the environment. And the best of the right fences is the one that is easy on the upkeep.

### Regional Style

But what about docks? What about dog houses and bird houses? What about adobe gardens, river rafts, hill houses, beach houses? What about bayous and fish-cleaning tables and ski racks; swimming holes and gazebos, house barns and fishing nets; granaries and island living? Much has been left out of this book that evokes specific locales. Country living varies widely in the different parts of the United States because this country is so vast and encompasses so many geographic and climatic zones.

Living Down Home is a purely personal affair. Only you know what you really want, and where you want it.

But what is Down Home? And where is it? Americans move, move, and move again, until many have no idea where home is anymore. People gravitate toward the country sometimes as if by instinct. Even if they don't fully understand their reasons for being there, they want it to feel like home.

This book has covered the basics of an approach to country living that is a truly American activity, the answer to a strong yearning for a quality of life that many people feel they once had. We hope it has demonstrated to you that all roads can lead Down Home.

*Twig furniture is an old craft and a current one. This twig end table sits next to an antique brown wicker chair on our country porch.*

*We lunch on our screened-in porch under a blue painted ceiling. Our table is set with Heisey glassware—an American favorite of mine—and garden flowers.*

From this Victorian wicker chair we sometimes watch the cardinals and the blue jays in the trees outside. While it is not particularly comfortable, the chair is a quality piece, and I keep it for its eye appeal.

This doorway leads to the second-floor bedroom of our country house. On the wall to the left of the door are two panels of American Indian arrowheads. The walls are painted Indian clay.

Weathered pine picnic tables sit on the rolling hills. We often use them for outdoor lunching. And sometimes we put them together for large birthday party gatherings.

Everyone seems to love the clay color of nature in brick walks and brick steps. And what is more appropriate on clay garden steps than a row of geraniums in clay pots?

*Window boxes should be filled with nature's color. It's early summer, and the one at our kitchen window is filled with pansies. I keep the flowers clipped so they will bloom all summer.*

253

*For the old fishing hole, turn a wooden watering trough into a bench.*

*Every Down Home barn needs a basketball hoop with backboard. A few panes of glass in the windows are broken, thanks to a shot or two that didn't make it. Allowance money helped repair the windowpanes, which are now protected with Down Home chicken wire.*

*Wood and stone are a perfect country combination. This X-designed fence is made of sturdy locust. The next time I photograph the fence, I hope it will be covered with purple-flowering clematis vine.*

*The Down Home barn is filled with treasures. Here, leaning against a stack of cedar shakes held in reserve for the next reroofing job, is an old wooden wheelbarrow filled with nested clay pots.*

Overleaf: *This bridge does not cross the River Quai; it crosses a trout stream in American country. Made by Reiss O'Neill of locust wood, the bridge has hand-carved front posts.*